HOW T ANYTHING ON EBAY

FOR BEGINNERS 2025

Ultimate eBay Selling Blueprint to Dominate Reselling, Retail Arbitrage and Product Flipping for Maximum Profits

ERIK S. TATUM

COPYRIGHT NOTICE

Table of Contents

Introduction

Welcome to Your eBay Selling Journey

Selling on eBay is a journey filled with opportunity, growth, and the potential to transform a simple idea into a thriving business. For anyone just stepping into this dynamic marketplace, the path may seem daunting at first, but it's also brimming with rewards for those willing to learn and adapt. The beauty of eBay lies in its versatility, catering to everyone from hobbyists looking to declutter their homes to ambitious entrepreneurs building an empire. Every successful seller starts somewhere, and your journey begins the moment you decide to explore the platform's vast possibilities.

eBay is more than just an online marketplace; it's a global stage where buyers and sellers meet to exchange products, ideas, and even dreams. With millions of active users worldwide, the platform offers unparalleled access to a diverse audience. This diversity means that almost anything can find a buyer if presented the right way. The key to success is understanding that eBay is as much about connecting with people as it is about selling products. Building trust and establishing a positive reputation are fundamental to creating a sustainable and profitable presence.

As a beginner, it's essential to approach this journey with curiosity and a willingness to learn. Success on eBay doesn't happen overnight, but each step forward builds the foundation for long-term achievements. Along the way, you'll discover what works best for you, from identifying profitable products to mastering the art of compelling listings. Mistakes will undoubtedly happen, but they are invaluable opportunities for growth. Each listing you create, each sale you make, and even each challenge you overcome will sharpen your skills and prepare you for greater success.

One of the most exciting aspects of selling on eBay is the ability to turn everyday items into sources of income. From household items you no longer need to discounted treasures found in local stores, the potential to profit is limited only by your creativity and determination. For those who embrace the thrill of discovery, sourcing products can become a passion in itself. Whether you're flipping thrift store finds or exploring retail arbitrage opportunities, eBay gives you the tools to turn effort into earnings.

As your journey unfolds, you'll realize that eBay is not just a platform but a learning experience. Every interaction, whether with buyers or within the seller community, adds to your knowledge and builds your confidence. You'll gain insights into customer behavior, pricing strategies, and the importance of communication. Over time, this understanding will transform you from a beginner into a seasoned seller capable of navigating the complexities of the marketplace with ease and expertise.

Your eBay journey is also a deeply personal one, shaped by your goals, interests, and vision for success. Some sellers aim to supplement their income, while others dream of replacing traditional jobs entirely. No matter your aspirations, eBay offers a flexible environment where you can work at your own pace and on your own terms. This flexibility, combined with the platform's global reach, makes it a unique and empowering opportunity for anyone willing to invest time and effort.

As you begin this adventure, remember that every great seller starts as a beginner. The path to mastery is not about rushing but about embracing the process and staying committed to your goals. Selling on eBay is a journey, not a destination, and each step forward brings you closer to the success you envision. With the right mindset, a willingness to learn, and a commitment to excellence, you have everything you need to thrive on eBay. Your journey has just begun, and the possibilities are endless.

Why eBay is the Perfect Platform for Beginners

One of eBay's most significant advantages is its immense global reach. With millions of active users worldwide, sellers gain instant access to a vast and diverse audience. For beginners, this means there is always potential demand for a wide range of products, from rare collectibles to everyday household items. This global marketplace offers a unique opportunity to tap into niches that might not exist locally. Additionally, eBay's reputation as a trusted platform helps instill confidence in buyers, making it easier for new sellers to establish credibility without having to build a brand from scratch.

The platform's flexibility in listing formats is another reason eBay is ideal for beginners. Sellers can choose between fixed-price listings, which are straightforward and predictable, and auction-style listings, which can generate excitement and competitive bidding. This versatility allows beginners to experiment with different selling strategies to find what works best for their products and target audience. eBay also accommodates sellers with varying inventory sizes, whether they are listing one-off items from their homes or managing a small business with consistent stock.

Another key factor is eBay's robust support system designed to help new sellers succeed. The platform provides a wealth of educational resources, including tutorials, webinars, and seller forums, where beginners can learn best practices and gain insights from experienced sellers. Additionally, eBay's customer service team is available to assist with technical issues, disputes, or questions, ensuring that sellers feel supported as they navigate the platform. These resources empower beginners to overcome challenges quickly, making the process of selling less daunting and more rewarding.

The financial benefits of selling on eBay are equally compelling for beginners. Since eBay does not require a significant upfront investment, sellers can start with items they already own, turning unused possessions into profit. This low-risk approach allows beginners to test the waters of online selling without significant financial pressure. Moreover, eBay's fee structure is transparent, with no hidden costs, enabling sellers to calculate their profits accurately and make informed decisions about their pricing and strategies.

Another aspect that makes eBay beginner-friendly is its built-in audience search functionality. The platform's algorithms ensure that listings are shown to buyers actively searching for similar items, which increases the chances of making a sale. Beginners can leverage eBay's search optimization tools, such as keywords and detailed descriptions, to improve their listings' visibility. Unlike creating and maintaining an independent online store, eBay simplifies the process of driving traffic to products, giving sellers more time to focus on improving their inventory and customer service.

Finally, eBay's adaptability to different seller goals makes it an ideal platform for beginners with varying aspirations. Some may start selling as a way to declutter their homes, while others may have ambitions of turning eBay into a full-time business. The platform supports both casual and professional sellers, providing the tools and resources needed to scale as their experience and confidence grow. This versatility ensures that beginners are not limited in their potential and can expand their operations as they gain expertise, turning eBay into a reliable and profitable venture.

How This Book Will Help You Master eBay Selling

This book is designed to be your ultimate guide to mastering eBay selling, especially if you're just starting out. Selling on eBay can feel overwhelming at first, with its vast marketplace, intricate policies, and ever-changing trends. However, this book simplifies the complexities, providing you with clear, actionable strategies to navigate the platform with confidence. It offers a step-by-step approach, taking you from understanding the basics to implementing advanced techniques, all aimed at helping you build a thriving eBay business. Whether you're selling a few items from your home or looking to establish a steady income stream, this book equips you with the tools you need to succeed.

One of the most valuable aspects of this book is its focus on product selection and sourcing. Finding the right products to sell is the cornerstone of success on eBay, and this guide explores deeply into how to identify profitable items, spot trending niches, and source inventory at low costs. It explores methods like retail arbitrage, thrift store hunting, and leveraging clearance sales to stock your virtual shelves with high-demand items. You'll learn to analyze market trends and buyer behavior, ensuring you always have products that appeal to your target audience. By mastering these techniques, you can turn small investments into significant returns.

Creating compelling listings is another area where this book will help you stand out. With millions of products available on eBay, crafting listings that grab attention is essential. This book teaches you how to write persuasive product descriptions, take professional-quality photos, and optimize your titles with relevant keywords. It also explains pricing strategies that balance competitiveness with profitability, giving you an edge over other sellers. By implementing these tips, you'll increase your visibility in search results and attract more buyers, boosting your sales and customer satisfaction.

Managing your eBay business efficiently is just as important as selling. This book provides insights into organizing your inventory, handling shipping logistics, and streamlining order processing to save time and reduce errors. It also introduces you to tools and software that can automate repetitive tasks, helping you focus on growing your business. From managing returns to responding to customer inquiries, you'll learn to handle every aspect of selling with professionalism and ease. These skills will not only help you maintain high ratings but also build a loyal customer base.

For those looking to scale their eBay operations, this book offers advanced strategies to grow your business. You'll discover how to expand your product range, enter new markets, and leverage eBay's promotional tools to maximize sales. It covers topics like running discounts, bundling products, and utilizing the global shipping program to reach international buyers. With these techniques, you can take your eBay business to new heights, transforming it from a side hustle into a full-fledged enterprise. The book emphasizes practical, proven methods that deliver results, no matter your starting point.

Additionally, this book prepares you for the challenges you may face as a seller. It identifies common mistakes beginners make and provides solutions to avoid them. From dealing with difficult customers to navigating eBay's policies, you'll learn how to overcome obstacles without jeopardizing your account or profits. The guidance provided ensures that you can tackle any issue with confidence, maintaining a positive reputation and minimizing setbacks. This focus on problem-solving is critical to long-term success in eBay's competitive marketplace.

Ultimately, this book is more than just a guide; it's a blueprint for creating a sustainable and profitable eBay business. By following the strategies outlined, you'll develop the skills, knowledge, and mindset needed to thrive as a seller. Whether your goal is to supplement your income, work from home, or build a scalable business, this book gives you the foundation to achieve it. With dedication and the right approach, you'll be well on your way to mastering the art of selling anything on eBay and maximizing your profits.

Chapter 1: Understanding eBay Basics

Setting Up Your eBay Account

Setting up an eBay account is the foundation of your journey to selling anything successfully on the platform. The process begins by creating a personal account or upgrading to a business account, depending on your goals. For individuals selling casually or testing the waters, a personal account suffices. However, if your vision involves scaling your operations and establishing a brand, a business account offers added features such as the ability to use a company name, access advanced selling tools, and benefit from detailed analytics. Regardless of your choice, the registration process requires a valid email address, a secure password, and essential personal or business details, including your name, address, and phone number. eBay also requests bank account information to facilitate smooth payouts, a critical step ensuring you can receive funds from your sales efficiently.

Once your account is created, verifying your identity is crucial. eBay emphasizes trust and transparency between buyers and sellers, and account verification plays a vital role in achieving that. Verifying your email address is a simple yet mandatory step, and linking your account to a valid phone number provides additional security. Sellers also need to set up eBay's managed payments system by providing their banking information and verifying it. This system streamlines the process of receiving payments and ensures that sellers receive their earnings directly into their bank accounts. Taking these steps not only secures your account but also reassures potential buyers that you're a legitimate seller.

Personalizing your profile enhances your credibility and makes your account more appealing to buyers. This includes adding a clear and professional profile picture, writing a concise and engaging bio, and listing any relevant details about your selling expertise. While it may seem minor, these details help build trust with your audience. Buyers often review seller profiles before making a purchase, and having a polished, professional appearance sets you apart from others. Consistency between your profile and the types of products you plan to sell further reinforces your legitimacy as a seller.

Familiarizing yourself with eBay's selling policies is an essential part of setting up your account. Understanding the rules surrounding prohibited items, intellectual property rights, and listing standards can save you from potential account restrictions or suspensions. It's important to read through eBay's guidelines thoroughly to ensure your practices align with their requirements. Additionally, knowing about fees such as insertion fees, final value fees, and optional promotional fees will help you budget effectively and price your items competitively while keeping profitability in mind.

To prepare your account for selling, you'll need to link a valid payment method for paying fees and other selling-related costs. Options include linking a debit or credit card or using PayPal if it's available in your region. Setting this up ensures uninterrupted selling activity, as eBay deducts its fees automatically. Furthermore, it's a good idea to enable two-factor authentication for an added layer of security. With this in place, even if someone attempts to access your account, they'll be unable to proceed without the unique code sent to your phone.

Once your account is ready, practicing with a few low-risk sales can help you get comfortable with the platform's interface and tools. Selling personal items, such as unused gadgets or clothes, allows you to gain firsthand experience without significant risk. These initial transactions can also help you build positive feedback on your account, which is essential for establishing credibility. Buyers on eBay pay close attention to seller ratings and reviews, and a strong feedback score can directly impact your sales volume and success.

Navigating the eBay Marketplace

The eBay marketplace is a dynamic environment where millions of buyers and sellers interact daily, making it a prime platform for beginners to start their selling journey. Understanding its structure and functionality is crucial to navigating it successfully. At its core, eBay functions as a digital marketplace that connects buyers with items they desire and sellers with potential customers. For a beginner, it is essential to familiarize yourself with the categories, search functions, and filters that eBay provides, as these tools can greatly impact the visibility of your listings and your ability to find profitable niches.

A fundamental aspect of eBay is the search algorithm, known as Cassini, which determines how listings are displayed to buyers. Cassini prioritizes listings based on relevance, quality, and engagement metrics such as views, clicks, and sales. As a seller, your goal is to optimize your listings so they rank higher in search results. Factors like a compelling title, detailed descriptions, high-quality images, competitive pricing, and positive feedback all play a role in enhancing your visibility. The better you understand how Cassini works, the more effectively you can position your items for success in the marketplace.

eBay offers two main types of selling formats: auctions and fixed-price listings. Auctions are ideal for items with uncertain value, allowing buyers to bid and determine the final price, which can sometimes exceed your expectations. Fixed-price listings, on the other hand, are straightforward and cater to buyers who prefer immediate purchases. Knowing when to use each format is a strategic decision that can influence your profits. For beginners, starting with fixed-price listings can help you gain stability and predictability as you learn the ropes of selling.

The marketplace also offers robust tools for managing your transactions, including options for accepting payments, setting shipping preferences, and handling returns. eBay primarily uses PayPal and other integrated payment solutions, ensuring secure and seamless transactions for both buyers and sellers. As a seller, you must be transparent about your shipping methods, estimated delivery times, and return policies to build trust and encourage repeat business. Clear communication and reliability in these areas can significantly enhance your reputation on the platform.

One of the most important aspects of navigating the eBay marketplace is understanding the competition. eBay is a vast marketplace with sellers from all over the world, so it's essential to research competitors who are selling similar products. Analyze their pricing, listing quality, shipping options, and feedback to identify opportunities for differentiation. Offering unique value, whether through better prices, faster shipping, or superior customer service, can help you stand out and attract more buyers.

Feedback is the currency of trust on eBay. Buyers rely heavily on seller ratings and reviews to decide whom to purchase from. As a beginner, prioritizing excellent customer service is vital to earning positive feedback. Prompt responses to inquiries, accurate product descriptions, fast shipping, and addressing any issues professionally can help you build a strong reputation. Over time, a high feedback score will boost buyer confidence, improve your search rankings, and increase your chances of repeat sales.

Finally, staying adaptable and informed about eBay's policies and updates is essential for long-term success. The platform frequently evolves to enhance user experience and maintain marketplace integrity, which means sellers must keep up with changes in listing requirements, fee structures, and seller performance standards. By remaining proactive and committed to learning, you can navigate the eBay marketplace with confidence, turning it into a reliable source of income and growth.

eBay Seller Policies and Fees

eBay seller policies and fees are central to building a successful eBay business. Understanding these components ensures that you can operate within eBay's rules while maximizing your profits. Seller policies on eBay are designed to create a fair and reliable marketplace. These policies govern various aspects of selling, such as product listings, delivery, returns, and buyer interactions. As a seller, you are expected to accurately describe your items, ensuring titles, descriptions, and images match the actual product. Misleading information can result in account restrictions or even suspension. It's also important to comply with prohibited and restricted item policies to avoid listing products that violate eBay's rules or legal regulations. Familiarizing yourself with these guidelines helps you steer clear of potential disputes or penalties.

eBay prioritizes customer satisfaction, so sellers are required to maintain high standards of service. This includes timely shipping and clear communication with buyers. Providing accurate tracking information and delivering items within the stated time frame is crucial. Late shipments or inconsistent updates can lead to negative feedback, affecting your seller rating. Managing returns effectively is another key aspect of eBay's policies. While you can set your own return policy, it's often advantageous to offer flexible options to attract more buyers. However, even if you don't offer returns, eBay's Money Back Guarantee ensures buyers are protected in cases of misrepresentation or item issues, so resolving disputes promptly and professionally is in your best interest.

eBay's fee structure can seem complex at first but becomes manageable with a clear understanding. There are two main types of fees: insertion fees and final value fees. An insertion fee is charged when you list an item, and it depends on the number of listings and the categories chosen. eBay often provides sellers with a set number of free listings per month, which is beneficial for beginners. Beyond the free threshold, insertion fees are calculated based on the category and quantity of listings. Final value fees are charged once your item sells. This fee is a percentage of the total transaction, including the item price and shipping cost, but excluding taxes. The percentage varies by category, with most being around 12 to 15 percent. Being aware of these fees allows you to price your items strategically, ensuring your desired profit margin is maintained.

eBay also offers optional upgrades for listings, such as bold fonts, additional images, or promoted listings to increase visibility. While these features can enhance sales, they come at an additional cost, so using them selectively and within your budget is important. Sellers using eBay Stores, a subscription-based option, benefit from discounted fees and tools to manage their inventory and branding more effectively. Choosing the right store plan depends on your sales volume and business goals, making it crucial to evaluate whether this option aligns with your needs.

Tax compliance is another important consideration. eBay collects and remits sales tax on behalf of sellers in many regions, but understanding your local tax obligations ensures you avoid surprises. Staying informed about eBay's periodic updates to their fee structure and seller policies is equally important. Changes can impact your bottom line, so regularly reviewing announcements and updates will help you adapt quickly. By maintaining compliance with eBay's policies and planning for fees, you position yourself for long-term success as an eBay seller, building trust with buyers while maximizing profitability.

Chapter 2: Finding the Best Products to Sell

The Power of Product Research

To find hot items, the first step is to immerse yourself in the buyer's perspective. Think about trends in the current market and what might be driving consumer interest. For instance, seasonal products often perform exceptionally well because they align with immediate needs or events. During the holidays, items like decorations, gift sets, or winter apparel become top sellers, while summer might bring demand for outdoor equipment, swimsuits, and travel gear. Being attuned to these cycles is a powerful way to anticipate what will sell before the competition saturates the market.

Researching eBay itself is an invaluable strategy. The platform provides plenty of tools to help you identify trends. One of the most effective is the "Completed Listings" and "Sold Listings" filter. By searching for a product and examining items that have already sold, you can see which products are in demand, what buyers are willing to pay, and even details like popular price points and listing formats. This data gives you a solid foundation for choosing items that are likely to sell. It's also important to pay attention to products that don't sell. If you notice a pattern of listings for a certain item ending without sales, that's a clear indication to steer clear.

Another essential part of the process is leveraging external tools to broaden your research. Platforms like Google Trends can provide insights into what people are searching for across the internet. You can track whether interest in a specific product is rising or falling, which can help you avoid investing in items that are losing popularity. Other tools, such as Terapeak (integrated into eBay) or third-party software, offer detailed analytics on trending products, pricing history, and other valuable data points. These tools may seem overwhelming at first, but they're incredibly helpful for making informed decisions rather than relying on guesswork.

Understanding your niche is also crucial. Many sellers find success by focusing on specific categories rather than trying to sell everything under the sun. For example, if you're passionate about electronics, you may already have an advantage because you understand what makes certain gadgets appealing or valuable. Your personal knowledge can guide you toward the products buyers are most likely to want. Selling in a niche allows you to build expertise, which translates into more accurate product descriptions, better customer service, and ultimately higher sales.

It's also worth mentioning the importance of sourcing the right products. Just because something is in demand doesn't mean it will generate profit if you can't acquire it at the right price. Retail arbitrage, where you buy discounted items from local stores or online retailers to resell on eBay, is a popular and accessible method for beginners. Clearance sections, thrift stores, garage sales, and even platforms like Facebook Marketplace can be treasure troves for finding undervalued items. The key is to assess whether the price you're paying allows room for profit after factoring in eBay fees, shipping costs, and any additional expenses.

Staying ahead of trends often requires thinking outside the box. Pay attention to social media platforms, where influencers frequently shape consumer behavior. Platforms like TikTok and Instagram can provide early clues about products that are about to become wildly popular. For example, a particular gadget, kitchen tool, or fashion item may start trending due to a viral video, and sellers who move quickly can capitalize on the surge in demand before others catch on.

Another strategy for finding hot items is keeping an eye on eBay's competitors. Amazon's bestseller lists, for instance, are a goldmine of information. While not every product that sells well on Amazon will be a hit on eBay, there is often significant overlap. Comparing what's trending on multiple platforms can help you identify universal demand, giving you a better chance of success.

Listening to your buyers can also be a game-changer. Pay attention to the questions and feedback you receive from customers. Sometimes, buyers will express interest in a product you don't currently sell, and their input can guide your future sourcing decisions. eBay itself offers buyer demand insights for certain categories, which can further help you understand where opportunities lie.

The most successful eBay sellers understand that product research is not a one-time task but an ongoing effort. The market is constantly shifting, with new trends emerging and old ones fading away. Sellers who commit to staying informed and adapting to these changes will consistently outperform those who rely on outdated or static strategies. By being proactive and resourceful, you can ensure that your store is always stocked with products that buyers are eager to purchase. In the end, the power of product research lies in its ability to transform your eBay store into a destination for high-demand items, setting you up for success and profitability.

How to Spot Profitable Niche Markets

To begin this process, start by thinking about what interests you. Selling items in a niche you are passionate about not only makes the process enjoyable but also gives you a deeper understanding of what potential buyers are looking for. Your personal knowledge can guide you toward the kinds of products people want and help you spot opportunities that others might overlook. For example, if you're a fitness enthusiast, you might notice the rising demand for specific types of resistance bands, yoga accessories, or wearable fitness technology. This type of insight can provide a solid foundation for choosing a niche.

Once you have a general idea of what interests you, it's time to dive into research. eBay itself is a powerful research tool. Spend time browsing through completed listings to identify what's selling and for how much. Pay attention to the number of bids on auction listings or the frequency of sales for Buy It Now items. These details can give you a clear picture of what buyers are actively purchasing. Keywords are also crucial during this stage. Search for terms related to your potential niche and examine the search results. If you see products with consistent sales, competitive pricing, and a manageable number of sellers, you may have found a promising niche.

Competition is an essential factor to consider. While high demand is great, it loses its value if the market is oversaturated with sellers. You want to find a niche with enough interest to generate consistent sales but not so much competition that it's impossible to stand out. One way to gauge competition is by looking at the top sellers in your chosen category. Study their listings to understand what they are doing well. Look at their product descriptions, pricing strategies, and feedback from buyers. This analysis will help you identify gaps you can fill, whether through better customer service, unique product variations, or more competitive pricing.

Another valuable source of information is trends. Trends often dictate what sells best on eBay, and keeping an eye on them can help you stay ahead of the curve. Platforms like Google Trends, Pinterest, and social media are excellent resources for spotting emerging interests. For example, if a particular product is gaining popularity on TikTok or Instagram, it's likely to see increased demand on eBay as well. Jumping on these trends early can help you establish a presence in a niche before it becomes saturated. However, it's important to balance trend-based products with evergreen items that have consistent demand over time. Relying solely on fleeting trends can make your sales unpredictable and limit your long-term growth.

While researching, don't underestimate the power of looking outside eBay for inspiration. Brick-and-mortar thrift stores, clearance sections, garage sales, and estate sales are treasure troves for potential niche products. Sometimes, the most profitable niches come from products that aren't immediately obvious but hold hidden value. For instance, vintage or collectible items often have a dedicated audience willing to pay a premium. If you can identify products in this category that others might pass over, you can carve out a unique space for yourself.

Once you've identified a promising niche, testing is the next crucial step. You don't need to go all in right away. Start small by listing a few items within your chosen niche and observing how they perform. Pay close attention to buyer interest, feedback, and sales velocity. This experimentation allows you to fine-tune your approach without overcommitting to inventory that might not sell. Over time, as you gather more data, you'll be able to make informed decisions about expanding your product line or refining your niche further.

In addition to testing, building relationships with your buyers is an often-overlooked strategy for niche sellers. Engaging with your audience through thoughtful communication and personalized service can turn one-time buyers into repeat customers. When people know you consistently provide value in a specific niche, they are more likely to return to your store whenever they need related products. Over time, this loyalty can create a steady revenue stream and reduce the need to constantly attract new buyers.

Ultimately, spotting profitable niche markets requires a blend of curiosity, research, and adaptability. By focusing on areas where you can offer unique value and understanding the dynamics of demand and competition, you can create a successful eBay business that stands out in even the most competitive markets.

Sourcing Products {Where and How to Find Them}

Sourcing products is the foundation of a successful eBay business. It's the process of finding items to sell that not only resonate with buyers but also maximize your profits. The key to sourcing effectively lies in understanding where to look and how to evaluate the potential of each product you come across. Many beginners get overwhelmed at this stage, but it doesn't have to be complicated. The opportunities to source products are vast and varied, ranging from physical locations to online platforms, each offering unique advantages depending on your goals, resources, and level of expertise.

One of the best places to start is your own home. Many eBay sellers begin their journey by selling items they no longer need. This could include old electronics, clothing, books, or household goods. By starting with things you already own, you get a chance to learn the ropes without any upfront investment. You'll gain experience in creating listings, shipping items, and managing customer interactions, all while decluttering your space. Once you've exhausted the items in your home, it's time to look outward.

Thrift stores, garage sales, and estate sales are treasure troves for unique and undervalued items. These places often have products priced far below their actual market value, making them ideal for flipping on eBay. The key is to develop a keen eye for what sells. Vintage clothing, branded shoes, limited-edition collectibles, and discontinued electronics are just a few examples of items that can fetch high prices online. At thrift stores, it's important to take your time browsing and researching. With garage and estate sales, arriving early often gives you first pick, but visiting toward the end of the day might land you better deals, as sellers are more motivated to clear out remaining items.

Retail stores are another excellent source, particularly for retail arbitrage. This involves buying discounted items from big-box stores or outlets and reselling them at a profit. Clearance sections can be goldmines for brand-new products, especially seasonal items, toys, or electronics that are being phased out. Using apps and tools to compare in-store prices with eBay's sold listings can help you determine whether a product is worth buying. Retail arbitrage requires a bit more upfront investment compared to thrift stores, but the profit margins can be just as rewarding.

Online platforms have revolutionized the way sellers source products. Websites like Facebook Marketplace, Craigslist, and OfferUp allow you to find local deals without leaving your home. These platforms are often filled with sellers looking to offload items quickly, which can work to your advantage. Additionally, auction sites beyond eBay, such as GovDeals and Police Auctions, offer access to surplus goods, liquidated items, and even abandoned storage units. Winning items at these auctions often means acquiring bulk quantities at a fraction of their retail price, which can be split up and resold individually for higher profits.

Wholesale suppliers and manufacturers are excellent options for sellers looking to scale their eBay business. By purchasing products in bulk directly from suppliers, you can secure lower per-unit costs, which translates to higher margins. This method often works well for new products, such as private-label items or generic goods with broad appeal. However, working with wholesalers requires research to avoid scams and ensure you're dealing with legitimate businesses. Websites like Alibaba, SaleHoo, and Global Sources can connect you with reputable suppliers, but always start with smaller orders to test the quality before committing to large quantities.

Another exciting way to source products is by tapping into trends and seasonal demand. Pay attention to current events, pop culture, and industry news to identify products that are gaining popularity. Limited-edition merchandise tied to movies, sports events, or viral trends can sell rapidly at a premium if you get in early. Seasonal items like holiday decorations, winter gear, or summer essentials also perform consistently well. The trick is to plan ahead, sourcing these items months in advance when prices are low and competition is minimal.

Networking can also open doors to unique sourcing opportunities. Building relationships with local businesses, collectors, or even fellow eBay sellers can lead to exclusive deals. Some businesses may have excess inventory they're willing to sell at a discount, while collectors might part with valuable items for the right price. Attending trade shows, flea markets, or community events can expand your network and expose you to new sourcing options. The connections you build can become invaluable as you grow your eBay business.

Once you start sourcing products, it's essential to continuously analyze your efforts to ensure profitability. Tracking expenses, shipping costs, and final sale prices will give you a clear picture of what's working and what isn't. Not every product will be a winner, and that's okay. The important part is learning from each experience and refining your approach. Sourcing is as much about strategy as it is about effort. The more time you spend researching and experimenting, the better you'll become at identifying products with high potential.

The Secrets of Product Sourcing for Beginners

One of the most important aspects of sourcing is understanding what sells. You don't want to waste time or money on items that might sit on your shelves for months without a buyer. The key is to focus on demand. A good starting point is researching eBay's completed listings to identify trending products in categories that interest you. This gives you an idea of what's moving quickly and at what price point. Popular categories such as electronics, fashion, home goods, and collectibles are always in demand, but you should also consider niches where competition might be lower. Narrowing your focus helps you build expertise in specific areas, which can be advantageous when pricing, listing, and negotiating with buyers.

When starting, you don't need to invest heavily in inventory. Many successful sellers begin by looking around their own homes. Unused items, old gadgets, or clothes you no longer wear can be the perfect way to learn the ropes of selling. These items have no additional cost to you and can help you get comfortable with eBay's platform while generating your initial sales. Plus, you gain valuable experience in creating listings, taking product photos, and shipping orders—all critical skills for your business.

Once you've tested the waters, it's time to explore external sources. Thrift stores, garage sales, and flea markets are treasure troves for finding unique and undervalued items. These venues often have hidden gems that can be resold at a much higher price online. The secret lies in your ability to spot value. For example, a vintage jacket found at a thrift store for a few dollars could sell for ten times the price if it appeals to the right audience. Learning how to evaluate items and assess their resale potential is a skill that improves with practice. Start small, develop an eye for bargains, and take note of the types of products that yield the best returns.

Retail arbitrage is another fantastic sourcing strategy. This involves buying discounted or clearance items from retail stores and reselling them at a profit. Big-box retailers often have end-of-season sales or clearance racks filled with deeply discounted items. Scanning these products with a price-checking app can quickly reveal their resale potential. It's an effective way to source brand-new items that buyers often prefer over used ones. As a beginner, it's best to stick to smaller quantities until you're confident in a product's demand.

Online marketplaces like Facebook Marketplace, Craigslist, and even other sections of eBay itself can also be great sourcing platforms. Many people sell items below market value simply because they want to get rid of them quickly. Negotiation can play a big role here. When approaching sellers, a polite and confident attitude often results in better deals. Additionally, you can purchase items in bulk, as sellers are more likely to give you discounts for larger orders. Bulk buying reduces your cost per item, increasing your overall profit margin.

For those looking to scale their sourcing efforts, wholesale suppliers and liquidation sales offer an excellent opportunity. Wholesalers sell products in large quantities at discounted prices, allowing you to stock up on inventory for your eBay store. Liquidation sales, on the other hand, involve buying unsold or returned merchandise from retailers. These are often bundled into pallets and sold at a fraction of the retail price. While this method requires a larger upfront investment, it's an effective way to secure inventory in bulk and at a significant discount.

Networking is an underrated but powerful sourcing strategy. Building relationships with other sellers, store managers, or even private collectors can open doors to exclusive deals and insights into sourcing opportunities. Sometimes, simply letting people know you're an eBay seller can result in them offering you items they no longer need. Local business owners clearing out old stock or friends decluttering their homes can become valuable sources of inventory.

It's also important to stay creative and flexible in your sourcing approach. Trends can shift quickly, and what's popular today might not be in demand tomorrow. Staying informed about market trends and being willing to adapt your sourcing strategies will keep your inventory fresh and relevant. Seasonal products, for instance, can be highly profitable if you plan ahead. Stocking up on holiday decorations in the off-season or focusing on back-to-school supplies during summer can give you an edge over competitors.

Every successful eBay seller understands the value of consistency in sourcing. Making it a habit to source regularly ensures that you always have new inventory to list. Buyers are drawn to active sellers with fresh products, so the more you replenish your store, the more likely you are to attract repeat customers. As a beginner, focus on building a routine that works for you, whether it's visiting local thrift stores weekly, checking clearance sales, or browsing online marketplaces daily.

Lastly, patience and persistence are key. Not every sourcing trip will result in high-value finds, and not every product you list will sell immediately. But with time and experience, you'll develop a sharp instinct for sourcing profitable items. Start with small, manageable steps, keep learning from each sale, and remember that every successful eBay seller began where you are now. With dedication and the right strategies, you'll soon master the secrets of product sourcing and build a thriving eBay business.

Chapter 3: Mastering Retail Arbitrage and Reselling

Retail Arbitrage 101

Retail arbitrage is one of the most exciting and accessible ways to begin your eBay selling journey, especially for beginners. It's essentially the art of buying products at a lower price from one place and reselling them at a higher price to earn a profit. This concept may sound simple, but the strategies and opportunities within retail arbitrage are vast, making it a highly lucrative avenue when approached with the right mindset and techniques.

Imagine walking into a retail store and spotting an item on clearance that's marked down significantly. You check its price on eBay using your smartphone and realize it's selling for double or even triple the cost. That's the essence of retail arbitrage: finding undervalued items in the physical or digital world and leveraging eBay's global marketplace to connect them with buyers willing to pay more. The beauty of this approach lies in the endless sources of products, whether from clearance sections, seasonal sales, outlet stores, or even online retailers running discounts. The opportunities are everywhere once you start training your eyes to see them.

One of the keys to success in retail arbitrage is learning how to spot the right deals. Not every discounted item is worth your time or investment, and it's essential to focus on products that have a proven track record of selling well on eBay. This requires research and tools. Using eBay's sold listings feature, for instance, can help you identify items that are in demand. Simply search for the product you're considering, filter by sold listings, and review the prices and frequency of sales. This data-driven approach ensures you're not guessing but making informed decisions about what to buy and resell.

Timing also plays a critical role in retail arbitrage. Retailers often slash prices during specific seasons, holidays, or inventory clear-outs to make room for new stock. Post-holiday sales, for example, are a goldmine for finding deeply discounted items that people may still want months later. Similarly, as certain products go out of season, like winter coats in the spring or summer pool floats in the fall, you can scoop them up at a fraction of their original cost and hold onto them until demand rises again. This practice, often called seasonal arbitrage, can yield impressive profits for those willing to be patient.

While physical retail stores offer plenty of opportunities, the digital landscape has also become a thriving arena for retail arbitrage. Websites like Amazon, Walmart, and Target frequently run sales and clearance events, allowing you to source products without leaving your home. Many successful eBay sellers utilize these online deals to stock up on items they know will sell for more on eBay. To stay competitive, some sellers use tools like price-tracking apps or browser extensions that alert them when specific products drop in price. These tools can be a game-changer, helping you act quickly on profitable deals before others catch on.

Understanding the psychology of buyers on eBay is another critical factor in maximizing your profits. People shop on eBay for various reasons, but one of the most common motivations is finding items they can't easily get elsewhere or snagging a great deal. When you list a product purchased through retail arbitrage, positioning it effectively can make all the difference. A well-crafted title, clear and attractive photos, and a detailed description that highlights the product's value can elevate your listing and attract buyers willing to pay a premium. Remember, you're not just selling a product; you're selling its perceived value, convenience, and sometimes even its rarity.

Another consideration is building your pricing strategy. It's tempting to undercut everyone else to secure a quick sale, but this isn't always the most profitable approach. Instead, focus on the unique aspects of your listing. For instance, if you're the only seller offering free shipping or fast delivery, you can justify pricing your item slightly higher than the competition. Buyers often prioritize convenience and reliability over saving a few extra dollars. As you gain experience, you'll learn how to find that sweet spot where your listings attract buyers while still maximizing your margins.

Inventory management is a challenge many beginners face, especially when they start finding more deals than they can handle. It's important not to overextend yourself by purchasing too much stock too quickly. Start small, test the market, and scale up as you gain confidence and experience. Focus on products you're familiar with or that resonate with a particular audience. This will make it easier for you to judge their value and understand your customers' needs. Keeping your inventory organized is just as crucial; knowing what you have, where it is, and how much it cost you helps streamline your operation and avoid costly mistakes.

One often overlooked aspect of retail arbitrage is the art of negotiation. While big-box stores may not allow for bargaining, smaller retailers, thrift stores, and clearance events often provide opportunities to negotiate prices further. Don't hesitate to ask for additional discounts, especially if you're buying in bulk. Every dollar saved on the sourcing side directly increases your profit margins.

Negotiation is a skill that improves with practice, so start small and grow your confidence over time.

Retail arbitrage also offers a surprising level of flexibility. You can start part-time, sourcing products during weekends or after work, and gradually expand as you see results. This makes it an ideal side hustle for beginners who want to dip their toes into the eBay selling world without making a full-time commitment. Over time, as you develop your skills and build a reliable income stream, you can decide whether to scale it into a more substantial business.

Finding Deals in Your Local Stores

Finding great deals in local stores is one of the most effective ways to source products for selling on eBay, and it can also be an exciting adventure once you know what to look for. The beauty of sourcing locally is that it opens up a treasure trove of opportunities that many people overlook. From clearance aisles in retail stores to hidden gems in thrift shops and garage sales, the possibilities are nearly endless if you know how to spot the right deals.

When you step into a store with the intent of finding items to resell, the first thing you need is a mindset shift. Instead of shopping as a consumer, start looking at items with a seller's eye. Ask yourself questions like, "What value does this item hold for someone else?"

and "Can I sell this at a profit?" Clearance sections are often the first place to start because they usually have items marked down to make room for new inventory. Retailers like Walmart, Target, or even your local grocery stores often have sections dedicated to discounted products. These items could include seasonal merchandise, discontinued items, or even packaging updates that leave older versions sitting on the shelf. Retail stores are constantly rotating stock, which means there's a steady flow of deeply discounted items ripe for reselling.

Thrift stores and charity shops are another goldmine for resellers. People donate items every day, which means you never know what treasures you'll find. From clothing and electronics to books and home goods, thrift stores are filled with items that may be undervalued locally but have significant appeal on eBay. The key is to learn how to evaluate the condition and market demand for these items. Some thrift stores even have sales days or discounts for certain categories, which can make your finds even more profitable. But timing matters; visiting these stores early in the day or on restocking days increases your chances of finding the best deals.

Garage sales and estate sales are also fantastic opportunities for finding deals. The sellers are often motivated to clear out space or get rid of items they no longer need, which means you can negotiate

prices to maximize your profit margins. People at garage sales are usually less concerned about making a profit themselves and more focused on getting rid of items quickly. This gives you room to negotiate while offering them a fair price. Estate sales, on the other hand, often have higher quality items but can still be an excellent source of products, especially for vintage or collectible goods.

Local discount outlets and liquidation stores can also be highly valuable resources. These stores often carry overstocked or returned items from big retailers at significantly reduced prices. You can find everything from electronics to home goods and even brand-name apparel. Since these items are often in new or like-new condition, they tend to perform well on eBay. Be prepared to spend time sorting through inventory, as not every item will be a winner, but the gems you do find can bring substantial returns.

Another overlooked strategy is shopping during specific times of the year when stores are more likely to have sales or discounts. For instance, after major holidays like Christmas or Halloween, stores heavily discount seasonal items to clear shelves. These products may not sell immediately, but they can be stored and listed on eBay when demand spikes again next season. Back-to-school and end-of-summer clearance sales are other opportunities to score high-demand products at a fraction of the cost.

Developing a system to check the value of items as you shop is essential. Using your smartphone to scan barcodes or search for similar products on eBay allows you to see what the item is currently selling for and whether it has consistent demand. This real-time research is critical for making informed purchasing decisions. Pay attention to the sold listings, not just the current ones, to get an accurate picture of an item's potential value. The more you practice this, the quicker you'll become at identifying profitable items on the spot.

Consistency is what will set you apart as a successful reseller. Regular visits to your local stores, whether it's weekly or biweekly, help you stay ahead of other resellers and catch new deals as they appear. Over time, you'll develop a keen sense of where to look, what to buy, and what to pass on. Every store has its unique rhythm when it comes to restocking and discounting, so building relationships with store employees can also give you an edge. Some employees may even tip you off about upcoming sales or when new clearance stock is being put out.

Using Online Tools to Source Products for Reselling

One of the first places to explore is online retail platforms. Websites like Amazon, Walmart, Target, and others often have deals, discounts, or clearance sections that can be goldmines for product sourcing. By using tools like price tracking software or deal-finding apps, you can identify items that are undervalued on these sites but have higher resale potential on eBay. The trick is to study price trends, look for items with a solid history of selling well, and buy them at a discount so you can flip them for a profit. Keep an eye out for seasonal discounts, flash sales, and limited-time offers that often make products even more lucrative for resellers.

Beyond retail websites, online auction platforms like eBay itself can be excellent sourcing grounds. Many people sell items on eBay at low starting bids, unaware of their actual value. By keeping a watchful eye on these listings, especially those with poor descriptions or inadequate photos, you can snag hidden treasures at bargain prices. Sniping tools, which allow you to place bids in the final seconds of an auction, can be incredibly useful for winning auctions without driving up the price too early. Additionally, searching for misspelled product names or vague titles often leads to listings with minimal competition, giving you a significant advantage.

Wholesale directories and websites are another invaluable resource. Sites like Alibaba, DHgate, and SaleHoo connect you directly to manufacturers and suppliers, often offering products at significantly lower costs. This approach is ideal for sellers who want to buy in bulk and maintain consistent inventory. However, the key to success here is building relationships with reliable suppliers and ensuring the products meet quality standards before committing to large purchases. Reading reviews, requesting samples, and starting with smaller orders can help mitigate risks and ensure a smooth reselling experience.

Dropshipping platforms provide an alternative for those who prefer not to hold physical inventory. Websites like Oberlo, Spocket, and even integration-friendly apps through Shopify allow you to source products from suppliers who handle storage and shipping on your behalf. While the margins might be lower compared to other sourcing methods, the reduced overhead and logistical simplicity make this an attractive option for beginners. It's crucial to research the reliability of your chosen dropshipping suppliers, as their performance will directly affect your reputation as a seller on eBay.

Social media platforms have become increasingly influential in product sourcing. Facebook Marketplace, for instance, is a hotspot for finding local deals on items people are eager to sell quickly.

Many sellers list items at low prices simply to declutter their homes, providing you with excellent reselling opportunities. Groups and forums dedicated to buying and selling, such as specialized resale or liquidation communities, also offer a wealth of opportunities for finding undervalued products. Similarly, platforms like Instagram and Pinterest can be used to identify trending items or niche products that are in high demand.

Data analysis tools designed specifically for eBay sellers can take your sourcing to the next level. Tools like Terapeak, Zik Analytics, and Jungle Scout help you analyze market trends, identify high-demand products, and assess the competition. They provide detailed insights into what's currently selling well on eBay, what prices are competitive, and how often specific products are being sold. By using these tools to guide your sourcing decisions, you can significantly increase your chances of success while avoiding products that may seem appealing but have limited market potential.

Liquidation and surplus websites like Liquidation.com and B-Stock are another excellent avenue for sourcing products. These sites offer pallets or lots of overstocked, returned, or refurbished items from major retailers. While this method requires an upfront investment and careful inspection of the lot details, the potential for profit is substantial, especially if you're comfortable selling items in various conditions. The key here is to understand the platform's bidding process, factor in shipping costs, and ensure the lot contents align with your target market on eBay.

You should also pay attention to global sourcing opportunities. Websites like AliExpress allow you to access international suppliers offering products at low costs. While shipping times may be longer, the savings on inventory can make it worthwhile, especially for items with consistent demand. By communicating directly with suppliers and negotiating terms, you can secure better deals and even establish long-term partnerships.

Reselling vs. Traditional Retail

Traditional retail is a familiar concept for most of us. It usually involves a physical or online store where you purchase products in bulk, often from manufacturers or wholesalers, to sell them at a markup. While this approach can seem appealing due to the structure and predictability it offers, it also comes with significant risks and barriers to entry. For starters, traditional retail often demands a substantial upfront investment. You might need thousands of dollars to stock inventory, rent storage space, or even set up a storefront. And then there's the issue of competition. In traditional retail, you're up against big players who can often offer lower prices due to economies of scale. As a beginner, these obstacles can feel overwhelming, even discouraging.

Reselling, on the other hand, flips the script in your favor. It's all about finding opportunities where others might not see them. You don't need to purchase massive amounts of inventory or secure expensive contracts with suppliers. Instead, you're sourcing products from everyday places—clearance aisles, thrift stores, garage sales, estate sales, or even your own attic. Think about it: there are countless items out there that people are willing to let go of at bargain prices, unaware of their true value on a platform like eBay. As a reseller, your job is to recognize that value and bring it to a marketplace where demand exists.

One of the biggest advantages of reselling is flexibility. You can start small, experimenting with a few items to see what works and what doesn't. This low-risk entry point is perfect for beginners who may not have a lot of capital to invest. Unlike traditional retail, where you're often locked into specific product lines or suppliers, reselling allows you to pivot quickly. If one category isn't working, you can easily shift to another without major losses. It's a level of adaptability that traditional retail simply doesn't offer.

Another aspect that makes reselling a better choice is how it aligns with modern consumer behavior. People love finding unique, second-hand, or hard-to-get items online. Whether it's a vintage T-shirt, a discontinued gadget, or a rare collectible, these are the kinds of products that thrive in the reselling market. Traditional retail often focuses on brand-new items that can be purchased from multiple outlets, making it harder to stand out. Reselling, on the other hand, gives you the chance to offer something distinct, something buyers can't easily find elsewhere.

There's also a community aspect to reselling that's hard to ignore. eBay is home to countless resellers who share their tips, tricks, and success stories. This sense of camaraderie can be incredibly motivating for beginners. Traditional retail can feel isolating, especially when you're navigating large supply chains and corporate negotiations. Reselling, however, invites you to be part of a vibrant, supportive network of sellers who understand the journey you're on.

One of the most exciting parts of reselling is the potential for high-profit margins. Imagine buying a rare book at a thrift store for a dollar and flipping it on eBay for fifty. That kind of return on investment is far less common in traditional retail, where your profit margins are often squeezed by supplier costs, shipping fees, and competitive pricing. Reselling gives you the ability to maximize profits by leveraging your knowledge, research skills, and a bit of creativity.

It's also worth mentioning how reselling on eBay fits seamlessly into a beginner's lifestyle. You don't need a warehouse or even a large amount of space to get started. Many successful eBay resellers operate right out of their homes, storing products in spare closets or garages. This convenience means you can scale at your own pace, adding more inventory as you become comfortable with the process. Traditional retail, by contrast, usually requires significant space and infrastructure from the very beginning, adding stress and financial strain to an already challenging endeavor.

Finally, let's talk about time and effort. Traditional retail often involves rigid schedules, from store hours to supplier meetings and inventory management. Reselling, especially on eBay, gives you control over your time. You can list items, process orders, and handle customer inquiries on your schedule, making it an ideal side hustle or even a full-time business for those seeking flexibility. This autonomy is one of the reasons so many people are drawn to reselling—it allows you to build a business that fits your life, not the other way around.

Chapter 4: Product Flipping

What is Product Flipping?

Product flipping is a straightforward yet highly effective strategy that involves buying items at a lower price and selling them for a profit. On eBay, this practice has become a cornerstone for sellers aiming to maximize their earnings, particularly for beginners who want to build a steady income stream. The concept revolves around identifying undervalued items or sourcing them at a discounted rate from various places such as clearance sales, thrift stores, garage sales, estate auctions, or even online platforms. The goal is to acquire products that hold resale value and can fetch a higher price when listed strategically.

The key to successful product flipping lies in understanding market trends and consumer demand. A product that seems ordinary to one person might be a highly sought-after item for someone else, creating an opportunity for profit. For instance, collectibles, vintage items, branded electronics, and even limited-edition merchandise often hold significant flipping potential. Researching these niches thoroughly and staying updated on what buyers are currently looking for on eBay can help sellers identify items with a strong resale value. Beginners should pay attention to eBay's completed listings feature, which provides insights into what similar items have sold for in the past, making it easier to estimate potential profits.

Timing also plays a crucial role in product flipping. Sellers must learn when to buy and when to list their items to optimize earnings. Some products, such as holiday-themed merchandise or seasonal items, have specific windows of opportunity where demand and prices peak. Understanding this cycle and listing items during high-demand periods can significantly enhance profitability. Additionally, finding items during off-peak seasons when prices are lower can provide a competitive advantage.

Condition is another critical factor that impacts product flipping success. Items in excellent or like-new condition tend to sell more quickly and at higher prices than those with visible wear and tear. When sourcing products for flipping, it's essential to evaluate their condition and determine if any cleaning, repairs, or restorations are necessary. These minor adjustments can often increase the item's perceived value, allowing sellers to command a higher price on eBay. However, it's important to weigh the costs of these improvements against the potential profit to avoid unnecessary expenses.

A successful product flipping strategy also requires effective pricing and listing techniques. Pricing should reflect the product's condition, rarity, and demand while remaining competitive within the eBay marketplace. Overpricing can deter potential buyers, while underpricing may leave money on the table. Crafting a compelling product description and including high-quality images can significantly influence buyer interest, as these elements help convey the item's value and authenticity. Transparency about the item's condition and any potential flaws also builds trust with buyers, increasing the likelihood of a successful sale.

Sourcing strategies are vital for beginners who want to excel in product flipping. Garage sales, for instance, often offer unique finds at rock-bottom prices. Many people hosting these sales are eager to clear out space and may not be fully aware of the resale value of their items, presenting excellent opportunities for flippers. Thrift stores and consignment shops are other valuable sources, especially for vintage clothing, books, and household goods that hold a niche appeal. Clearance sections in retail stores are prime spots for acquiring brand-new items at heavily discounted prices, ideal for flipping on eBay for a premium.

Beginners must also recognize that patience and persistence are necessary for product flipping success. Not every item will sell immediately, and some may require adjustments in pricing or relisting before they find the right buyer. Monitoring listings, analyzing market trends, and staying adaptable to changing consumer demands are part of the process. Over time, this approach helps sellers refine their sourcing and pricing strategies, improving their profitability with each transaction.

How to Flip Products from Garage Sales, Thrift Stores, and Clearance Sales

The process begins with knowing how to identify items with potential resale value. At garage sales, you'll often find hidden treasures at incredibly low prices because sellers are primarily looking to declutter rather than profit. Items such as vintage clothing, rare collectibles, electronics, books, and home decor are commonly undervalued but hold strong resale potential on eBay. To succeed, it's essential to develop a keen eye for valuable items by researching trends and understanding what sells well on the platform.

Thrift stores provide a consistent source of inventory, offering a wide array of secondhand goods at reasonable prices. These stores are particularly advantageous for finding high-quality items such as branded apparel, unique household items, and even discontinued products that can fetch a premium online. Clearance sales, often hosted by major retailers, are goldmines for acquiring new products at discounted prices. These items are appealing to buyers who prefer "like-new" or "new in box" listings. Retailers typically mark down overstock, end-of-season goods, or items with slight packaging flaws, giving resellers an opportunity to purchase products at a fraction of their original cost.

Success in flipping requires strategic purchasing decisions. Before making a purchase, it's crucial to conduct real-time market research on eBay. This can be done using eBay's completed listings feature, which reveals what similar items have recently sold for. By comparing the sale prices to the cost of acquisition, you can estimate potential profit margins and determine whether an item is worth buying. Mobile apps like the eBay app or barcode scanners make this process quick and efficient while you're on the hunt.

Condition is another critical factor when sourcing products. Items in excellent condition or with minimal signs of wear generally sell faster and for higher prices. For used items, ensure they are clean, functional, and free from major defects. When it comes to collectibles, authenticity is key, so it's essential to verify that items are genuine before listing them on eBay. Any flaws or imperfections should be clearly described in your eBay listings to build trust with buyers and avoid returns.

Pricing is a delicate balance that requires understanding market demand and buyer expectations. Competitive pricing strategies involve listing products slightly below average market value to attract more attention or, for rare items, setting a higher price point to reflect scarcity. Auctions can be a valuable tool for flipping unique or highly desirable items, as they encourage competitive bidding among buyers, often resulting in higher sale prices. Fixed-price listings, however, offer more control and are ideal for everyday items with steady demand.

Presentation plays a pivotal role in successful product flipping. High-quality photographs showcasing the item from multiple angles can significantly increase buyer interest. Providing detailed descriptions that highlight key features, brand names, and the item's condition ensures transparency and helps build buyer confidence. Adding relevant keywords to your title and description improves search visibility, making it easier for potential buyers to find your listings.

Efficient inventory management is essential as you scale your flipping operations. Keeping track of what you've purchased, how much you've spent, and the expected profit margins allows you to make informed decisions about future investments. Organizing your inventory in a way that makes it easy to locate items when they sell ensures smooth order fulfillment, which contributes to positive feedback from buyers.

Shipping is another aspect that requires careful consideration. Offering competitive or free shipping options can make your listings more attractive, but it's important to factor shipping costs into your pricing strategy to avoid cutting into your profits. Ensuring fast and reliable shipping services enhances buyer satisfaction and helps you build a strong reputation on eBay.

Learning from each transaction is a key component of mastering the art of flipping. Over time, you'll gain insights into which categories and items consistently yield high profits, allowing you to refine your sourcing strategies. Building relationships with regular sellers at garage sales or staff at thrift stores can also give you access to better deals and early information about new inventory.

Online Flipping Strategies for Maximum Profit

The first step in online flipping is learning to spot profitable opportunities. Conduct thorough product research using tools such as eBay's advanced search filters, Terapeak, or third-party apps like Zik Analytics. Search for items with high demand but limited availability, as these tend to fetch higher prices. Look for keywords like "clearance," "liquidation," "used," or "unclaimed returns" when browsing online marketplaces such as eBay itself, Amazon, Facebook

Marketplace, and Craigslist. Auctions on eBay can also yield hidden gems if you monitor listings with low starting bids or ending times during off-peak hours.

Understanding product niches is critical. Popular niches include electronics, vintage or collectible items, branded clothing, toys, and home goods. Beginners should focus on a niche they are familiar with or passionate about to make sourcing and selling more intuitive. Once you've identified a potential niche, study its market trends. Research the average sale prices of similar items and analyze completed eBay listings to understand what sells and at what price point. Be cautious of saturated markets where profit margins may be slim due to heavy competition.

Sourcing products for flipping is the next key step. Beyond traditional online marketplaces, consider exploring less obvious options like auction sites, liquidation websites, or government surplus platforms. These sources often sell items in bulk at a fraction of their retail value. Beginners should start small to test the waters, gradually scaling their operations as they gain confidence. It's crucial to factor in all costs, including shipping, storage, and eBay fees, to ensure your margins remain healthy.

Once you've sourced your products, creating high-quality listings is essential to maximize profit. Begin with a compelling title that includes relevant keywords potential buyers are likely to search for. Your product description should be concise but informative, highlighting key features, benefits, and the item's condition. Invest time in taking clear, well-lit photos that showcase the product from multiple angles. Buyers are more likely to trust listings with professional-grade images, even from amateur sellers.

Pricing your items strategically is another critical element. Conduct a pricing analysis by comparing similar listings and gauging buyer interest. Setting a competitive price can attract buyers quickly, but don't undervalue your items. Consider offering "Buy It Now" options for immediate purchases or auctions to spark bidding wars, particularly for rare or highly sought-after products. Additionally, offering free or discounted shipping can make your listing more attractive, as many buyers factor shipping costs into their purchasing decisions.

Marketing your listings can further amplify your sales potential. eBay provides tools such as promoted listings, which boost the visibility of your products in search results. Social media platforms are also valuable for driving traffic to your eBay store. Join relevant Facebook groups, Reddit communities, or forums related to your niche, but ensure your promotions are authentic and not overly sales-driven.

Providing value to these communities can establish your credibility and indirectly lead to more sales.

Another powerful strategy is bundling related items to create added value for buyers. For instance, grouping accessories with electronics or selling a complete set of collectible items can justify a higher price point. Similarly, targeting seasonal trends—such as selling holiday-themed items or back-to-school supplies—can significantly boost profits. Stay ahead of the curve by planning your inventory around upcoming events or holidays.

To truly maximize profits, optimize your backend operations. Efficiently manage your inventory to avoid overstocking or running out of high-demand items. Use spreadsheets or inventory management tools to track your purchases, sales, and profitability. Streamline your shipping process by pre-purchasing supplies, creating pre-packaged boxes, and using eBay's shipping discounts for cost savings. Timely communication with buyers and quick shipping can earn you positive feedback, which enhances your seller reputation and increases buyer trust.

Finally, scaling your online flipping strategy involves diversifying your product range and investing in higher-value items. As you gain experience, venture into sourcing luxury goods, limited-edition items, or refurbished electronics that yield higher returns. Building strong relationships with wholesalers, liquidators, or suppliers can give you access to exclusive deals, reducing your sourcing costs. Additionally, consider starting your own eBay store for increased credibility and branding opportunities.

Flipping for Beginners

The first step to successful flipping is developing a keen eye for value. This means learning to recognize items that are undervalued or have hidden potential. It could be something as simple as a vintage watch at a garage sale or a limited-edition collectible at a thrift store. Often, these items are overlooked by others because they don't immediately scream "profit," but with some research and intuition, they can become hidden gems. Research is your best friend in this process. Spend time on eBay studying what sells and for how much. Look at completed listings, not just current ones, to see what items consistently fetch a good price. This data gives you an idea of trends and helps you avoid investing in items that won't yield significant returns.

Once you've identified a potential item, sourcing becomes the next critical step. Sourcing involves finding these undervalued treasures at the lowest possible cost. Start small and local—visit garage sales, thrift stores, flea markets, and clearance racks. The beauty of flipping is that it doesn't require a huge initial investment. You can start with as little as a few dollars and gradually scale up. Clearance sections in retail stores are goldmines for flipping, especially for items that are still in demand but marked down due to overstock or seasonal changes. Similarly, estate sales and auctions can yield incredible finds if you're patient and willing to dig through what others might consider junk.

When you've sourced items, the next step is preparing them for sale. Presentation is everything on eBay, where buyers make decisions based on how an item looks in photos and how it's described in the listing. Clean and polish your items if necessary, ensuring they appear as appealing as possible. High-quality photos taken from multiple angles can make all the difference. Use natural lighting and uncluttered backgrounds to highlight the item. In your listing, be honest yet persuasive. Detail the features and benefits of the item while being upfront about any flaws. Transparency builds trust with potential buyers and reduces the risk of returns.

Pricing is another crucial aspect of flipping. It requires a balance between competitiveness and profitability. Research similar listings to find a pricing sweet spot, but don't undervalue your item just to make a quick sale. Many beginners fall into this trap, not realizing that strategic pricing can yield higher profits. For example, if your item is rare or in high demand, pricing slightly higher than your competitors can still attract buyers willing to pay a premium. Offering free shipping or bundling items can also make your listings more appealing without significantly cutting into your profit margins.

After listing your items, patience and adaptability come into play. Not every item will sell immediately, and that's okay. Monitor your listings and adjust as needed. Perhaps your price is too high, or the title isn't optimized with the right keywords. Sometimes, simply relisting an item with better photos or a more enticing description can make all the difference. Stay engaged with your inventory and be proactive about making improvements. Each adjustment brings you closer to a sale and teaches you something new about what works on eBay.

Once a sale is made, the process doesn't end there. Packaging and shipping your item with care ensures a positive experience for the buyer. Invest in sturdy packaging materials and consider the buyer's perspective when preparing their purchase for shipment. This attention to detail not only ensures safe delivery but also increases the likelihood of receiving positive feedback. A solid reputation on eBay is invaluable, especially for beginners looking to build trust and attract more buyers. Happy customers are often repeat customers, and their reviews can draw in new buyers as well.

Flipping is a skill that grows over time. The more you practice, the better you become at identifying valuable items, sourcing effectively, and maximizing profits. Don't be afraid to make mistakes along the way; each misstep is an opportunity to learn and refine your process. What starts as a simple side hustle can quickly grow into a reliable source of income or even a full-time business. The journey of flipping for beginners is one of discovery, persistence, and growth. Every item flipped brings you closer to mastering the art and building a sustainable eBay selling strategy that thrives on creativity and determination.

Chapter 5: Optimizing Your Listings for Maximum Exposure

Creating Listings That Sell

Creating a listing that sells is both an art and a science. On eBay, where competition is fierce, the way you present your item can make the difference between it sitting idle and being snapped up quickly. The foundation of a great listing lies in crafting an irresistible title and description that captures attention, sparks curiosity, and compels buyers to hit that "Buy Now" or "Bid" button.

The title of your listing is often the first thing potential buyers see. It needs to be clear, descriptive, and packed with relevant keywords that buyers are likely to search for. Think of it as the bait that draws people in. A vague or incomplete title will bury your listing among thousands of others, while a carefully thought-out title can propel it to the top of search results. Keywords are crucial because they connect your listing to the buyer's search query. When creating your title, imagine you're the buyer—what words would you type into the search bar if you were looking for this item? For example, instead of a generic title like "Sneakers," a more effective option would be "Nike Air Max 270 Sneakers, Size 10, Black/Red, Brand New." This title not only includes the product name but also provides essential details like size, color, and condition, making it easier for buyers to find your item.

Another important aspect of a great title is avoiding unnecessary words or symbols. While it's tempting to add phrases like "L@@K" or "WOW," these don't contribute to search relevance and can make your listing appear less professional. Stick to straightforward, keyword-rich titles that focus on what buyers need to know at a glance. If your item has a specific brand name, model number, or unique feature, be sure to include it in the title. These details often help your listing stand out and attract serious buyers.

Once the title has caught the buyer's attention, the description must seal the deal. This is where you get the chance to showcase your item in detail and build trust with potential buyers. A strong description doesn't just describe the item; it tells a story and answers questions before they're even asked. Buyers want to know exactly what they're getting, so clarity and honesty are key. Start by providing a complete overview of the item, including its condition, dimensions, materials, and any relevant features or specifications. For example, if you're selling a used laptop, mention details like the processor speed, memory capacity, operating system, and battery life. If there are any scratches, dents, or other imperfections, be upfront about them.

Buyers appreciate honesty and are more likely to trust a seller who provides a transparent description.

Tone is another critical element of your description. While it's important to be professional, don't be afraid to inject a little personality into your writing. A conversational tone can make your listing feel more approachable and relatable, which helps establish a connection with potential buyers. For example, instead of writing, "This is a used chair," you could say, "This comfy chair has been my go-to for years, and it's still in fantastic shape. It's perfect for anyone looking to add a cozy touch to their home." This kind of language humanizes your listing and makes it more appealing.

In addition to being informative and engaging, your description should be easy to read. Use short sentences and break up large blocks of text into smaller paragraphs. Buyers often skim through listings, so presenting information in a digestible format is crucial. Include all the important details early on to ensure buyers don't miss them. If your item has any unique selling points, such as being a limited edition or having special features, highlight these prominently in the description. These details can be the deciding factor for buyers who are comparing your listing to others.

One often overlooked aspect of crafting an effective description is anticipating buyer questions. Think about the kind of information you'd want to know if you were purchasing the item, and address those questions proactively. For example, if you're selling a collectible, mention whether it comes with its original packaging or any certificates of authenticity. If it's an item that requires assembly or additional accessories, let buyers know what's included and what they might need to purchase separately. By answering these questions upfront, you not only save time by reducing the need for back-and-forth messages but also build buyer confidence in your listing.

Keywords also play a role in your description. Just as with the title, including relevant keywords throughout your description helps your listing appear in search results. However, avoid keyword stuffing, as this can make your description hard to read and may even violate eBay's policies. Instead, integrate keywords naturally into your writing so they enhance the flow of your description rather than detract from it.

One of the final touches to a compelling description is a strong call to action. Encourage buyers to act by expressing urgency or emphasizing the value of your item. Phrases like "Don't miss out on this rare find!" or "Add it to your collection today!" can nudge buyers toward making a decision. While subtle, these prompts can create a sense of excitement and urgency that drives sales.

Photography Tips to Make Your Products Stand Out

1. **Use Proper Lighting**

    o   Natural light is your best friend. Take photos near a window during daylight hours to avoid harsh shadows and ensure even lighting.

    o   If natural light isn't available, invest in inexpensive softbox lights or a ring light to illuminate your product without creating glare.

    o   Avoid using your camera's flash as it can create harsh reflections and unnatural colors.

2. **Choose a Clean Background**

    o   A plain white or neutral background works best, as it minimizes distractions and focuses attention on the product.

    o   Use poster boards, white fabric, or even professional photography backdrops to create a clean and polished look.

o   Avoid cluttered or busy backgrounds that may confuse potential buyers.

3. **Take Multiple Angles**

   o   Show the product from every perspective, including the front, back, sides, top, and bottom.

   o   Highlight any unique features, details, or branding that make the product desirable.

   o   Capture close-ups of important elements, such as textures, patterns, or serial numbers.

4. **Display Size and Scale**

   o   Help buyers understand the product's dimensions by including a common object for reference, such as a coin, pen, or ruler.

   o   Alternatively, use a scale guide or label the photo with measurements for clarity.

5. **Capture Flaws or Imperfections**

   o   Be honest about the product's condition. If there are scratches, dents, or other imperfections, photograph them clearly.

o   Transparency builds trust and minimizes potential disputes with buyers.

6. **Stabilize Your Camera**

   o   Use a tripod to eliminate camera shake and ensure sharp, professional-looking photos.

   o   If you don't have a tripod, steady your hands or rest your camera on a solid surface while shooting.

7. **Use the Right Camera Settings**

   o   Most modern smartphones are equipped with high-quality cameras, which are sufficient for eBay photography.

   o   Enable gridlines to frame your shot symmetrically.

   o   Ensure your camera is set to the highest resolution and avoid using zoom, as it can reduce image quality.

8. **Stage Your Product Creatively**

   o   For lifestyle items, show the product in use. For example, display a mug on a table with coffee or a jacket being worn.

- o For functional items, illustrate how they solve a problem or serve their purpose.

- o Ensure staging feels authentic and doesn't misrepresent the product.

9. **Eliminate Reflections and Glare**

- o For shiny or reflective items like jewelry or electronics, angle the product slightly to avoid catching reflections of the photographer or surroundings.

- o Use a light diffuser or softbox to minimize glare.

10. **Edit Your Photos Thoughtfully**

- o Use simple editing tools to adjust brightness, contrast, and sharpness.

- o Crop out unnecessary background space to focus attention on the product.

- o Avoid over-editing, which can distort the product's true appearance and mislead buyers.

11. **Optimize Image Size for eBay**

   o eBay recommends images at least 1600 pixels on the longest side to ensure high-quality viewing on all devices.

   o Save photos in JPEG format for quick loading without sacrificing quality.

12. **Include a Gallery Image**

   o Your first image (gallery photo) should be the most visually appealing and informative.

   o It's the first thing buyers see when browsing, so make it count with a clean, well-lit shot of the product.

13. **Avoid Distracting Elements**

   o Remove unnecessary props unless they serve to enhance the product's appeal or context.

   o Ensure the entire product fits within the frame and remains the main focus of the photo.

14. **Label or Watermark Strategically**

   o If you want to protect your images, add a subtle watermark that doesn't obscure the product.

- o Avoid using overly large or bold text, as it can distract from the product itself.

15. **Test Different Shots**

   - o Experiment with angles, lighting setups, and arrangements to determine what works best for your product.

   - o Compare different photos and choose the ones that make the product look most attractive.

Setting the Right Price

The first step in pricing is research. eBay offers a treasure trove of information for sellers who know where to look. One of the most valuable tools available is the "Sold Listings" filter. By searching for items similar to what you're selling and filtering to see recently sold items, you can discover the average price buyers are willing to pay. This data provides real-world insight into what the market currently supports. Pay attention not only to the sale price but also to the condition of the item, whether it was new or used, and any additional factors like shipping costs. This research phase ensures that your pricing aligns with buyer expectations while staying competitive.

Understanding how buyers perceive value is also critical. Buyers on eBay are often looking for deals, but that doesn't mean they always go for the lowest price. Factors such as your seller rating, the quality of your photos, and the detail in your description can justify a slightly higher price. A professional-looking listing signals to buyers that they're dealing with a trustworthy seller, which can make them more willing to pay a premium. However, if you're a beginner without a solid track record of positive feedback, you may need to price slightly lower initially to build credibility and attract your first few buyers.

The timing of your listing can also play a role in pricing strategy. Some sellers prefer auction-style listings, which can generate excitement and drive up the price if multiple bidders are interested. However, auctions can be risky because they may end with a lower-than-expected final price, especially if there's limited interest in your item. Fixed-price listings offer more control and predictability, allowing you to set a price that reflects the value of your item. eBay also offers the "Best Offer" option, which can be a powerful tool for engaging buyers who might otherwise pass on your listing. With this option, buyers feel empowered to negotiate, and you can still maintain control over the minimum price you're willing to accept.

Shipping costs are another critical factor that influences pricing. Many buyers consider the total cost, including shipping, when deciding whether to purchase an item. Offering free shipping can make your listing more attractive, but you need to account for this cost in your pricing to avoid cutting into your profits. Alternatively, you can offer a flat-rate shipping fee or calculated shipping based on the buyer's location. Whichever method you choose, transparency is key. Buyers appreciate knowing upfront what they'll pay without encountering surprises at checkout.

Seasonality and trends can also impact pricing decisions. Certain products may sell for higher prices during specific times of the year. For example, holiday decorations are in high demand leading up to Christmas, while outdoor gear tends to sell better in the spring and summer. Staying attuned to these seasonal fluctuations allows you to adjust your pricing to maximize profits. Similarly, keeping an eye on market trends can help you capitalize on hot-selling items and avoid overpricing products that have lost their appeal.

Psychological pricing techniques can be a subtle yet effective way to influence buyer behavior. Pricing an item at $19.99 instead of $20 can make it feel like a better deal, even though the difference is minimal. These small adjustments can have a big impact on how buyers perceive the value of your listing. Additionally, creating a sense of urgency by mentioning limited stock or time-sensitive discounts can encourage buyers to act quickly, reducing the likelihood that they'll compare prices with other sellers.

Building flexibility into your pricing strategy is another important consideration. Market conditions can change quickly on eBay, especially for popular items. A product that sells for a premium one month may see increased competition and lower prices the next. Regularly reviewing your active listings and comparing them with competitors ensures that your pricing remains relevant and competitive. This might involve adjusting prices downward to match the competition or raising them if you notice an uptick in demand.

While setting the right price is essential, it's equally important to ensure that your costs are covered. Many beginners overlook hidden expenses like eBay fees, PayPal fees, and packaging materials, which can eat into profits if not accounted for. Calculating your total cost per item, including shipping and fees, allows you to determine a minimum price that ensures profitability. Once you've established this baseline, you can decide how much higher to price your item based on market research and perceived value.

Pricing isn't a one-size-fits-all strategy, and what works for one seller may not work for another. Experimentation is key. Over time, you'll develop a better understanding of how different factors influence buyer behavior and what pricing strategies work best for your specific products. The more data you collect and analyze, the more confident you'll become in setting prices that attract buyers while maximizing your profits.

Shipping Strategies

The first thing to understand about shipping is that the way you package your items reflects directly on you as a seller. Buyers are often excited about receiving their orders, and the presentation of the package can make a lasting impression. Use sturdy materials, such as durable boxes and bubble mailers, to protect your items during transit. If you're shipping fragile goods, take extra precautions by adding cushioning like bubble wrap, packing peanuts, or even shredded paper to absorb any impact. Ensure that items are tightly packed to minimize movement within the box. Clear labeling also helps avoid mishandling, so always make sure your shipping label is legible, securely attached, and includes all necessary information. When buyers receive an item in excellent condition, they are more likely to leave positive feedback, which boosts your reputation.

Choosing the right shipping carrier is another essential step in building a reliable shipping process. eBay offers a variety of carrier options, including USPS, UPS, FedEx, and international services.

Each carrier has its strengths, so you should select one based on the size, weight, and destination of your package. For lightweight items, USPS First-Class Mail is often the most cost-effective choice, while heavier packages may be better suited for UPS or FedEx Ground. For valuable or time-sensitive items, consider expedited shipping options like Priority Mail or Express Shipping. Researching and comparing rates can help you minimize shipping costs, which is important for maintaining profitability.

Shipping speed is a top priority for many buyers, so offering multiple shipping options can make your listings more attractive. Some buyers are willing to pay extra for expedited delivery, while others may prefer a slower, more economical option. By providing a range of choices, you allow customers to select the shipping method that best fits their needs. eBay's estimated delivery dates play a crucial role in buyer satisfaction, so be honest and realistic when setting your handling time. A shorter handling time, such as same-day or one-day processing, can boost your visibility in search results and increase buyer confidence. However, it's vital to ensure you can consistently meet the commitments you set. Overpromising and underdelivering can lead to negative feedback and disputes.

Another factor to consider is the use of tracking information. Providing buyers with a tracking number is not just a best practice;

it's often expected. Tracking offers peace of mind to both you and the buyer by allowing both parties to monitor the package's progress. Most carriers offer tracking as part of their service, but double-check to ensure it's included, especially for international shipments. Once the package has been shipped, upload the tracking number to eBay as soon as possible. This transparency reassures buyers and reduces the likelihood of disputes or inquiries about the package's whereabouts.

International shipping opens up a world of opportunity, but it also comes with its challenges. Buyers from different countries can significantly expand your customer base, but navigating customs, duties, and shipping regulations requires extra attention. eBay's Global Shipping Program simplifies this process by handling customs clearance and international delivery on your behalf. All you need to do is ship the item to eBay's domestic hub, and they take care of the rest. If you choose to manage international shipping independently, research each destination country's restrictions and customs requirements. Properly completing customs forms and declaring the package's contents accurately can prevent delays and ensure a smooth delivery experience.

Communication with your buyers throughout the shipping process is an underrated yet essential part of offering speed and reliability.

Once an item is shipped, let the buyer know it's on its way and share the tracking details. If there are any unexpected delays, be proactive in informing the buyer and providing updates. Buyers appreciate transparency, and clear communication can turn a potential complaint into a positive experience. Prompt responses to any shipping-related inquiries also demonstrate your commitment to excellent customer service.

Another way to enhance your shipping strategy is by taking advantage of eBay's discounted shipping labels. eBay partners with major carriers to offer sellers reduced rates, which can save you money while still providing reliable service. Printing shipping labels directly through eBay is not only cost-effective but also convenient, as it automatically updates the order status and tracking information for the buyer. This streamlined process saves time and minimizes errors.

Insurance is another consideration for sellers, especially when shipping high-value or fragile items. While most carriers include basic insurance for their services, you may need to purchase additional coverage for items that exceed their limits. Insurance protects both you and the buyer in case of loss or damage during transit. If an issue arises, you'll have the necessary protection to resolve it without absorbing the full cost.

Consistency is the key to building trust with your buyers. When buyers know they can rely on you to ship their items quickly and safely, they are more likely to return for future purchases. Reliable shipping practices also encourage positive reviews and ratings, which play a significant role in attracting new customers. Over time, your ability to deliver a smooth, hassle-free shipping experience will become one of the pillars of your eBay business.

Finally, never underestimate the power of little extras to delight your buyers. Including a thank-you note or a small freebie can leave a lasting impression and encourage repeat business. While these gestures aren't necessary, they show your customers that you value their purchase and are willing to go the extra mile.

Chapter 6: The eBay Seller's Toolbox

Essential Tools for eBay Sellers

Product Research Tools

Understanding market trends and identifying profitable products is the foundation of successful eBay selling. These tools can help you find winning products:

- **Terapeak Product Research** (Available in eBay Seller Hub): Provides insights into sales trends, pricing strategies, and market demand for products.

- **Zik Analytics**: A powerful tool to research best-selling items, analyze competitors, and identify high-demand, low-competition niches.

- **Google Trends**: Tracks product seasonality and consumer interest over time, helping you decide when to source specific items.

Listing Optimization Tools

Creating compelling and optimized product listings is crucial for visibility and sales. These tools simplify the process:

- **Canva**: A user-friendly design tool for creating professional-looking images, logos, and banners to enhance your brand.

- **eBay's Listing Tool**: Available within the Seller Hub, this tool helps you create, edit, and optimize your listings with features like bulk editing and auto-suggested categories.

- **Keywords Everywhere**: A browser extension that helps you identify relevant keywords for your titles and descriptions, ensuring your listings are SEO-friendly.

Inventory Management Tools

Keeping track of your inventory is key to avoiding overselling or stockouts. These tools make inventory management seamless:

- **SkuGrid**: Tracks supplier inventory and pricing changes and updates your eBay listings automatically.

- **Sellbrite**: Helps manage inventory across multiple marketplaces (eBay, Amazon, Etsy), ensuring your stock levels stay accurate.

- **eBay's Inventory Management Feature**: Simplifies inventory tracking directly on the platform and integrates with other tools.

Pricing and Profitability Tools

Setting the right price is critical for attracting buyers while ensuring profitability. Use these tools for accurate pricing and cost management:

- **Profit Bandit**: Calculates your potential profit after fees, helping you decide whether a product is worth selling.

- **eProfit**: A mobile app that tracks costs, fees, and margins, allowing you to monitor profitability in real time.

- **PriceYak**: Automates price adjustments based on competitor activity, ensuring you stay competitive.

Order and Shipping Management Tools

Streamlining the order fulfillment and shipping process is vital for providing excellent customer service. These tools ensure fast and reliable deliveries:

- **ShipStation**: Integrates with eBay to manage shipping labels, track orders, and find the best shipping rates.

- **Pirate Ship**: Offers discounted USPS rates, helping you save money on shipping.

- **AfterShip**: Tracks shipments and notifies buyers of delivery status, enhancing the customer experience.

Customer Service and Feedback Management Tools

Maintaining excellent communication and managing feedback are essential for building a positive seller reputation:

- **Replyco**: Centralizes messages from eBay buyers, enabling fast and professional responses.

- **Feedback Genius**: Automates feedback requests and helps manage buyer reviews to maintain high ratings.

- **Zendesk**: A customer service platform that integrates with eBay, allowing you to handle inquiries efficiently.

Automation and Workflow Tools

Automation tools help reduce manual workload and scale your eBay business more effectively:

- **AutoDS**: Automates dropshipping tasks like product imports, price updates, and inventory monitoring.

- **iMacros for eBay**: A browser extension that automates repetitive actions, such as relisting or adjusting prices.

- **eBay Selling Manager Pro**: eBay's native tool for automating listing renewals, generating sales reports, and tracking performance.

Accounting and Financial Tracking Tools

Accurate accounting is critical to tracking profits and preparing for taxes. These tools simplify financial management:

- **QuickBooks Online**: Tracks income and expenses, generates invoices, and simplifies tax preparation.

- **GoDaddy Online Bookkeeping**: Syncs with eBay and PayPal to track sales, fees, and profits automatically.

- **Wave**: A free accounting tool perfect for small sellers to manage finances.

Mobile Apps for On-the-Go Selling

Staying connected to your eBay business while on the move is crucial. These apps ensure you're always in control:

- **eBay App**: Enables you to list items, respond to buyer messages, and monitor sales from your smartphone.

- **PayPal App**: Tracks payments and refunds efficiently (if you're still using PayPal).

- **Scanner Apps (like Scoutify or Inventory Lab)**: Helps scan barcodes in stores for retail arbitrage, providing instant pricing and profitability data.

Analytics and Performance Tracking Tools

Analyzing your sales performance is key to identifying strengths and areas for improvement:

- **eBay Seller Hub Performance Tab**: Tracks sales metrics, conversion rates, and customer insights directly on eBay.

- **DataHawk**: Offers advanced analytics for monitoring sales trends and competitor activity.

- **InventoryLab**: Tracks profits, expenses, and ROI, offering in-depth performance reports.

Managing Inventory and Sales with Ease

Managing inventory and sales on eBay is a skill that often separates successful sellers from those who struggle to keep up. As a beginner, it's easy to overlook the importance of staying organized, but this is the backbone of building a sustainable eBay business. When you know exactly what you have in stock, where it is, and how quickly it's selling, you can operate with confidence, avoid costly mistakes, and focus on growing your profits.

At the core of managing inventory effectively is creating a system that works for you. It doesn't have to be complex, but it does need to be consistent. Even if you're only selling a handful of items at first, keeping track of each product is essential. You don't want to find yourself in a situation where a customer places an order for an item you no longer have because it was misplaced or accidentally sold elsewhere. That's a quick way to damage your seller rating and credibility. Start by assigning a designated storage area for your inventory, whether it's a small corner of your home, a set of shelves, or bins with clear labels. Group similar items together, and always place them back in the same location after taking photos or preparing them for shipping. The idea is to develop a habit where you always know exactly where everything is.

Tracking your inventory digitally is another important step in managing your eBay business with ease. You can use spreadsheets, apps, or specialized inventory management software. At its simplest, a spreadsheet can include columns for item descriptions, quantities, purchase dates, and selling prices. If you prefer something more robust, there are affordable tools available specifically designed for eBay sellers that can automate much of the process. These tools not only track your inventory but can also sync with your eBay account to update listings automatically when items sell or go out of stock. This eliminates manual updates and reduces the risk of overselling, especially if you're managing multiple listings.

As you begin to sell more items, keeping an eye on sales trends becomes crucial. Some products will naturally sell faster than others, and recognizing these patterns early allows you to adjust your strategy. For instance, if a particular item consistently sells out quickly, it's worth sourcing more of it to keep up with demand. Conversely, if an item has been sitting unsold for weeks or months, it might be time to discount it or reconsider whether it's worth listing in the future. The goal is to maintain a healthy balance of fast-moving items that generate steady cash flow and higher-margin products that might take a little longer to sell but deliver significant profits when they do.

Shipping supplies should also be considered as part of your inventory. Having an organized system for packaging materials like boxes, bubble wrap, tape, and labels ensures you're always ready to fulfill orders promptly. Running out of supplies at the last minute can delay shipments and lead to frustrated buyers. It's wise to stock up on these essentials and store them alongside your inventory for quick access. Many eBay sellers even invest in thermal label printers and scales to streamline their shipping process, saving both time and money in the long run.

Communication with buyers plays an indirect but vital role in managing sales. Prompt responses to inquiries, clear communication about shipping times, and follow-ups after a sale all contribute to a positive customer experience. When buyers feel valued and informed, they're more likely to leave positive feedback, which directly impacts your reputation as a seller. A good reputation attracts more buyers and increases sales, creating a cycle of success.

Returns and refunds are inevitable in any business, but how you handle them can make or break your eBay journey. Having a clear return policy and addressing issues professionally can turn a potentially negative experience into an opportunity to showcase your excellent customer service. Keep track of returned items, inspect them thoroughly, and decide whether they're suitable for resale or need to be written off. Managing returns efficiently ensures your inventory remains accurate and helps you minimize losses.

Another aspect to consider is the importance of staying organized during peak sales periods, such as holidays or promotional events. These times can bring a surge in orders, and being unprepared can lead to chaos. Planning ahead by increasing your inventory levels, streamlining your workflow, and setting realistic expectations for shipping times can help you handle the pressure and maintain customer satisfaction.

Scaling your eBay business often means diversifying your inventory and expanding into new product categories. As you add more items, the complexity of managing your inventory naturally increases. Regular audits become necessary to ensure your records match your actual stock. Periodically review your listings to confirm that quantities, prices, and descriptions are accurate. An organized inventory system not only saves time but also allows you to focus on tasks that grow your business, like sourcing new products and refining your sales strategies.

Automating Your eBay Business for Maximum Efficiency

The first step to automating your eBay business involves understanding the tools and features that eBay itself provides. eBay offers seller tools like the Seller Hub, which is a centralized platform to manage your listings, sales, and performance metrics. It allows you to schedule listings in advance, automatically relist items that haven't sold, and set up templates for repetitive tasks such as creating new product descriptions. Using templates alone can save hours of work every week, especially when you're selling similar types of products or operating in a specific niche. Another helpful feature is the ability to automate pricing adjustments. With eBay's promotional tools, you can set discounts to run during specific time frames or use tools like markdown sales to attract buyers without having to manually change your prices.

Beyond eBay's native features, third-party tools can take your automation efforts to the next level. Inventory management software is particularly valuable for sellers juggling multiple products. Tools like InkFrog, Sellbrite, or GoDaddy Online Bookkeeping integrate seamlessly with eBay and allow you to track your inventory, avoid overselling, and get alerts when stock levels run low. With these tools, you can synchronize your inventory across multiple platforms if you're selling on other marketplaces like Amazon or Etsy, making it easier to keep everything in order. Similarly, shipping software like ShipStation or Pirate Ship can be a game-changer, enabling you to print shipping labels in bulk, calculate shipping costs instantly, and streamline the entire shipping process. These tools also provide tracking information that can be automatically sent to buyers, reducing the number of customer inquiries you'll have to manage.

Automating customer service is another crucial element of creating efficiency in your eBay business. Responding to buyer messages and resolving issues can be time-consuming, especially as your sales volume grows. By setting up eBay's automatic response templates, you can address common questions quickly and professionally. For instance, you can create a template that provides details about your return policy or estimated delivery times. Automation doesn't mean neglecting your buyers; it means offering them timely, consistent communication while freeing up your time for more critical tasks.

Additionally, using feedback management tools can help you request feedback from buyers automatically, ensuring that you maintain a strong seller reputation without constantly monitoring it yourself.

Order fulfillment is another area where automation can make a significant impact. Many beginners start by packing and shipping orders manually, but this process can quickly become overwhelming as your sales increase. Fulfillment services like Fulfillment by Amazon (FBA) or third-party logistics providers can handle your inventory storage, packing, and shipping for you. While there are costs associated with these services, the time you save can be reinvested into growing your business. Alternatively, if you prefer to manage shipping yourself, automating label creation and bulk shipping processes can help streamline the workflow and reduce errors.

Dynamic pricing tools are also an excellent way to automate and optimize your eBay business. Pricing is a critical factor in attracting buyers, but manually adjusting prices to stay competitive can be time-consuming. Automated repricing tools analyze market trends, competitor prices, and your profit margins to adjust your prices automatically. This ensures that your products remain competitive without you constantly having to monitor the market. Tools like

RepricerExpress or PriceYak are designed to help you stay ahead in a competitive marketplace while maximizing your profits.

Automating marketing and promotion is another powerful strategy for efficiency. eBay's Promoted Listings feature allows you to set up advertising campaigns that run automatically, boosting your visibility in search results. You can choose a budget and let the system handle the rest, displaying your items to potential buyers who are actively searching for similar products. If you have an email list or social media following, tools like Mailchimp or Hootsuite can help you automate outreach and social media posts, ensuring that you maintain a consistent online presence without needing to manually create content every day.

One of the less obvious but highly effective ways to automate your eBay business involves setting up workflows for repetitive tasks. Many sellers find themselves bogged down by mundane activities like responding to the same types of messages or updating inventory spreadsheets. With tools like Zapier, you can create workflows that connect different apps and automate these processes. For instance, you can automatically add new sales to a spreadsheet or trigger a shipping notification email whenever an order is marked as shipped. While setting up these workflows might require some initial effort, they can save you countless hours in the long run.

It's important to note that while automation is incredibly useful, it's not about removing the human element from your business entirely. Automation is a way to handle repetitive and time-consuming tasks so that you can focus on areas that require your expertise, such as finding profitable products and building relationships with buyers. When balanced correctly, automation can give your eBay business the structure and efficiency it needs to thrive without compromising the quality of your customer experience.

Lastly, as you begin to implement automation in your business, it's crucial to track and evaluate its effectiveness. Automation tools are designed to save time and increase profitability, but they can also create inefficiencies if not set up properly. Regularly reviewing your processes and making adjustments as needed will ensure that your automated systems continue to work in your favor. By embracing automation, you'll not only make your eBay selling journey smoother but also position yourself for long-term success in the competitive world of online reselling.

Chapter 7: Growing Your eBay Store

How to Scale Your eBay Business Quickly

One of the most effective ways to grow is by expanding your product catalog. A limited inventory can restrict your sales potential, so it's essential to diversify. Consider sourcing new items from wholesale suppliers, clearance sales, or even global markets. The more variety you offer, the broader your appeal to different buyers. However, it's not just about quantity; quality matters even more. Ensure that every item in your store meets or exceeds customer expectations, as one bad review can overshadow ten good ones. Balancing this act of scaling up inventory while maintaining high standards will establish you as a trusted seller, which is crucial for sustained growth.

Another key element in scaling is optimizing your listings. The way you present your products can make or break a sale. High-quality photos with multiple angles, clear and engaging descriptions, and keywords that align with what buyers are searching for will ensure that your listings stand out. eBay's search engine heavily favors well-crafted listings, and this is where you can gain a significant edge over competitors who might not put in the same effort. If buyers can instantly see the value and quality of your product, they're far more likely to purchase, and repeat sales often follow.

Pricing strategies also play a pivotal role in scaling quickly. Competitive pricing doesn't necessarily mean offering the lowest price; instead, it's about offering the best value. This could involve bundling products, offering discounts for bulk purchases, or even using promotions to attract first-time buyers. Experimenting with auctions can also be a great way to draw attention to your listings. While fixed-price listings might feel safer, auctions often create urgency among buyers, leading to higher-than-expected final sale prices.

Customer service is a non-negotiable factor in scaling. Satisfied customers not only return but also spread the word, often bringing in new buyers. Fast response times, clear communication, and resolving issues proactively build trust and loyalty. Offering benefits like free shipping or hassle-free returns can also differentiate your store from competitors and encourage customers to shop with you over others. Many sellers underestimate the power of maintaining a stellar reputation. Each positive review and high seller rating significantly contributes to how eBay's algorithm ranks your listings, giving you more visibility and, ultimately, more sales.

Leveraging eBay's tools and programs is another critical aspect of rapid growth. Features like eBay's Promoted Listings allow you to pay for additional exposure, which can be a game-changer for new sellers looking to get their products in front of more buyers. Similarly, the Global Shipping Program opens up international markets, enabling you to reach millions of potential buyers worldwide without dealing with the complexities of international shipping yourself. Taking advantage of these built-in tools can help you gain momentum faster than relying solely on organic growth.

Building relationships with suppliers is an often-overlooked way to scale efficiently. Reliable suppliers ensure that you always have stock, and negotiating better terms with them as your business grows can lead to increased profit margins. Strong supplier relationships also give you access to exclusive deals or hard-to-find items, which can set your store apart from others. The ability to consistently offer unique or in-demand products creates a sense of anticipation among your buyers, keeping them coming back for more.

Technology can be your best friend when scaling an eBay business. Automation tools can save you time and reduce errors, allowing you to focus on strategic growth. For instance, inventory management software helps track stock levels and prevents overselling, while analytics tools provide insights into what's working and what isn't.

The more data-driven your approach, the easier it becomes to identify opportunities for improvement. Additionally, outsourcing tasks like shipping or listing management can free up your time to focus on higher-level decisions that drive growth.

Building a Brand on eBay

The foundation of a strong eBay brand lies in consistency. Every aspect of your store should reflect a unified theme or style, from the tone of your product descriptions to the layout of your store. Your product images should maintain a consistent aesthetic, with clear, high-quality photos that use similar backgrounds and lighting. This not only creates a professional look but also gives buyers the impression that you are an organized, trustworthy seller. Over time, these small touches build familiarity, and repeat customers will begin to recognize and trust your brand based on this consistency.

Customer service plays a significant role in defining your brand. The way you interact with buyers, handle inquiries, and resolve issues contributes to the reputation you build over time. Responding promptly and politely to messages signals that you value your customers. Similarly, maintaining clear and fair return policies shows buyers that you stand behind the products you sell. Many sellers underestimate how much of an impact positive customer experiences can have on building a brand. Satisfied buyers are not only more likely to leave positive feedback but may also recommend your store to others or return for future purchases.

Your eBay listings are another crucial component of your branding strategy. Descriptions should not just provide product details but should also reflect your brand's personality. Whether your tone is professional and straightforward or friendly and conversational, it's important to use a voice that aligns with the image you want to project. Titles should be clear, informative, and optimized with keywords buyers are likely to search for. This approach not only improves visibility but also ensures your listings appeal to the right audience.

Pricing strategies also contribute to how buyers perceive your brand. Competitive pricing can attract budget-conscious shoppers, but offering value is just as important. This doesn't always mean having the lowest price; it could mean offering free shipping, bundling products together for a better deal, or including small extras that enhance the buyer's experience. Buyers often equate added value with professionalism and trustworthiness, which strengthens your brand.

Your feedback score and seller ratings are, in many ways, the lifeblood of your eBay brand. Buyers rely heavily on these metrics to determine whether or not they feel comfortable making a purchase.

Ensuring that you maintain a high level of satisfaction across transactions is critical. This includes not only fulfilling orders accurately and promptly but also being proactive about resolving disputes or complaints. A small act, like offering a partial refund for minor inconveniences, can go a long way in showing that you prioritize customer satisfaction. Over time, a solid feedback profile becomes synonymous with your brand's reliability.

Visual identity extends beyond just your store logo and photos. Many successful eBay sellers invest in custom templates for their listings to create a uniform, professional look. Templates can include personalized headers, consistent formatting, and even branding elements like your logo or tagline. These details help make your store stand out and give buyers a sense of familiarity as they browse through your listings. They reinforce the idea that you are running a serious business rather than casually selling items on the side.

Another often overlooked aspect of branding on eBay is the packaging of your products. The moment a buyer receives their order, your brand's impression is either reinforced or weakened. Using clean, secure packaging, branded materials like thank-you cards, or even small promotional inserts can leave a lasting positive impression. Buyers are far more likely to remember you and return for future purchases when they feel appreciated. This level of thoughtfulness can differentiate you from other sellers offering similar products.

Marketing efforts off-platform also contribute to your eBay brand's visibility and strength. Sharing your eBay store on social media, creating a website that links to your listings, or running promotions through email campaigns can help establish your presence beyond eBay's marketplace. These strategies allow you to attract more buyers, many of whom may never have found your store otherwise. Expanding your reach reinforces the legitimacy of your brand and can significantly increase your sales.

Expanding Your Product Line

One of the first things to focus on when adding new categories is understanding your current customer base and their interests. Analyzing the products you're already selling successfully can reveal patterns that indicate what else your buyers might want. For instance, if you're currently selling sports equipment, expanding into related categories like fitness accessories or outdoor gear could be a natural and profitable transition. Customers who trust your products in one category are more likely to shop with you again if they see you offering complementary items. This cross-selling approach builds customer loyalty and increases the average order value.

Research plays a crucial role in identifying which categories to add. Start by exploring trending products within different niches on eBay. You can use tools like eBay's "Trending" section, Google Trends, or third-party software designed for product research to pinpoint items that are currently in demand. Pay attention to seasonal trends as well, as they can offer lucrative opportunities if you time your listings right. For example, winter might be an ideal time to introduce categories like holiday decorations or thermal wear, while summer could be perfect for outdoor and travel-related items. Expanding into categories with proven demand ensures you're not venturing blindly and increases the likelihood of a successful transition.

When you begin to expand, it's essential to ensure that the new categories align with your brand identity, even if you're just starting out. A cohesive and professional-looking eBay store builds trust and credibility among buyers. Adding too many unrelated categories at once can confuse potential customers and dilute your store's overall appeal. For instance, if your store has been focused on selling home decor items, suddenly listing car parts might feel out of place and deter loyal customers who were drawn to your original niche. Maintaining a consistent theme while gradually branching out into related areas ensures that your expansion feels natural and well thought out.

As you add new categories, sourcing becomes an essential part of the equation. It's not enough to simply decide what to sell—you need reliable suppliers who can provide high-quality products at competitive prices. Explore local wholesalers, online marketplaces like Alibaba, or even retail arbitrage opportunities to find the right inventory for your new category. Building strong relationships with suppliers ensures you have a steady flow of products and minimizes the risk of stockouts, which can harm your seller ratings and customer trust. Diversifying your sources can also help you navigate supply chain challenges and give you more flexibility in pricing and product availability.

Once you have your new inventory, presentation is key. Every new category you introduce should be backed by high-quality listings that showcase the products in their best light. This means writing detailed, keyword-rich descriptions that highlight the unique features and benefits of each item. High-resolution photos that capture multiple angles and details of the product are essential for building buyer confidence. Don't underestimate the power of a well-optimized listing; it can make the difference between a customer choosing your product or moving on to a competitor's.

Expanding your product line also requires you to stay organized. Managing multiple categories can quickly become overwhelming if you don't have a system in place. Consider using inventory management tools to keep track of stock levels, sales performance, and shipping logistics across all your categories. A well-organized operation not only reduces stress but also ensures that your customers receive their orders promptly and accurately, which is critical for maintaining positive feedback and repeat business.

Marketing is another crucial aspect of successfully adding new categories. Once you introduce a new range of products, you need to let your audience know about it. Use eBay's promotional tools, such as discounts, coupons, and bundled offers, to draw attention to your new items. You can also leverage social media platforms to reach potential buyers who may not yet be familiar with your eBay store. Sharing posts, creating targeted ads, or engaging with niche communities online can generate interest in your expanded product offerings and drive traffic to your listings.

Customer feedback is invaluable as you expand your product line. Pay attention to reviews, questions, and messages from buyers about your new categories. This feedback can provide insights into what's working and what needs improvement. If you notice recurring issues or suggestions, address them promptly to enhance your offerings and show your customers that their opinions matter. Building a reputation for being responsive and attentive can set you apart from other sellers and foster long-term loyalty.

Finally, patience and adaptability are critical during this process. Expanding your product line is not an overnight success story; it requires trial and error, learning from mistakes, and constantly refining your approach. Some categories may perform better than others, and that's perfectly normal. By analyzing your sales data and staying attuned to market trends, you can continue to adjust your strategy, ensuring that your eBay business grows in a sustainable and profitable way. Each new category you add brings an opportunity to learn, grow, and ultimately dominate the marketplace in ways you hadn't imagined before.

Managing Your Reputation

Managing your reputation on eBay is one of the most critical aspects of building a successful and sustainable business. As a beginner, you might underestimate how much your reputation influences potential buyers' decisions, but it's one of the first things shoppers look at before making a purchase. A strong reputation makes you appear trustworthy and professional, while a poor one can deter even the most interested customers. The foundation of your reputation on eBay revolves around three pillars: customer service, feedback, and handling returns effectively. These elements work together to not only secure repeat business but also attract new buyers who feel confident purchasing from you.

Providing exceptional customer service is where everything begins. On eBay, your interaction with customers often occurs through messages. The tone and speed of your responses can leave a lasting impression. Prompt responses to inquiries, even when the questions seem trivial, show buyers that you value their time and business. It's also important to remain polite and professional, especially when dealing with difficult customers. Instead of seeing complaints as a challenge, consider them opportunities to demonstrate your willingness to resolve issues. By maintaining a calm and helpful demeanor, you can turn a potentially negative experience into a positive one, which might even lead to glowing feedback.

Your listings themselves are an extension of your customer service. Clear and honest descriptions reduce the likelihood of misunderstandings or disputes later. Buyers appreciate when sellers provide detailed information about products, including any flaws or imperfections. Adding high-quality images from multiple angles is equally important. These practices not only help buyers make informed decisions but also show that you prioritize transparency. Transparency builds trust, and trust strengthens your reputation. When buyers feel they've received exactly what they were expecting, they're more likely to leave positive feedback, which is essential for establishing credibility as a new seller.

Feedback is the currency of trust on eBay. As a beginner, every positive review you receive is a step closer to becoming a top-rated seller. However, earning positive feedback requires consistent effort. After completing a transaction, it's a good idea to politely request feedback from your buyers. Many will leave reviews without prompting, but a courteous message thanking them for their purchase and inviting them to share their experience can increase your chances. Keep in mind that the way you handle challenges also plays a significant role in the feedback you receive. If something goes wrong, addressing the issue swiftly and professionally can often prevent negative feedback. Buyers understand that mistakes happen, but how you resolve them matters most.

Negative feedback can feel like a major setback, especially when you're just starting out, but it's not the end of the world. The first step is to evaluate the situation objectively. If the feedback is valid, reach out to the buyer and offer a solution. Sometimes, offering a partial refund, replacement, or another gesture of goodwill can prompt the buyer to revise or remove their negative feedback. If the feedback violates eBay's policies, such as being abusive or factually incorrect, you can report it for removal. Building a positive feedback record takes time, but staying proactive and consistently providing great service will help you overcome any bumps along the way.

Returns are another area where your reputation can be significantly impacted. While no seller enjoys dealing with returns, they're an inevitable part of doing business on eBay. The key is to make the process as smooth and hassle-free as possible for the buyer. Offering a clear and fair return policy from the outset is essential. Buyers appreciate knowing that if something goes wrong or the item doesn't meet their expectations, they have options. When a return request comes in, respond quickly and courteously, even if the situation feels frustrating. Remember, how you handle returns not only affects the buyer involved but also your overall reputation on the platform.

One of the biggest mistakes new sellers make is taking return requests personally. It's easy to feel frustrated when a buyer claims an item wasn't as described or arrives damaged, but staying calm and professional is critical. Begin by reviewing the buyer's explanation and any evidence they provide. If the issue was your fault, such as an error in the listing or inadequate packaging, take full responsibility and work to resolve it. Even if the buyer is at fault or the issue seems minor, maintaining a polite and accommodating approach is the best way to protect your reputation.

The eBay platform rewards sellers who consistently provide a positive experience for their customers. Top-rated sellers gain access to benefits such as increased visibility in search results and discounts on final value fees. Achieving and maintaining this status requires a strong commitment to customer satisfaction. This means not only responding to inquiries and handling returns effectively but also going above and beyond whenever possible. Small gestures, such as including a thank-you note with the item or offering discounts to repeat customers, can leave a lasting impression and encourage buyers to leave glowing reviews.

Chapter 8: Advanced Selling Strategies

Using eBay Promotions and Discounts to Drive Sales

When you consider eBay promotions, think of them as a way to boost visibility and appeal. Promoted Listings is one of the most powerful tools at your disposal. By opting to promote your listings, you can position your products at the top of search results, giving them a better chance of being seen by potential buyers. The cost for this service is performance-based, meaning you only pay a small fee if the item sells through the promoted listing. For beginners, this is a low-risk way to test the waters and learn how visibility impacts your sales. As your experience grows, you can fine-tune your promotion strategy by choosing which items to promote, focusing on high-margin products or those with strong demand.

Discounts, on the other hand, are an excellent way to create irresistible offers that buyers find hard to ignore. eBay's Markdown Manager allows you to set up sales events where you can offer discounts on one or more items in your store. You have full control over the percentage off and the duration of the sale, giving you flexibility to test different approaches. Buyers are naturally drawn to the appeal of a good deal, and a product that's marked down can often feel more valuable simply because of the perceived savings. Offering discounts is not just about reducing your price—it's about making your offer look compelling in comparison to your competitors' listings.

Another effective tool is the Best Offer feature. This allows buyers to negotiate the price with you, giving them a sense of control over the transaction. While some sellers shy away from this feature, fearing lowball offers, it can be an excellent way to attract buyers who are looking for flexibility. Accepting reasonable offers or countering with fair prices can help you close sales faster. It's important to stay professional and strategic when using this feature; every negotiation is a chance to turn a potential buyer into a loyal customer.

Coupons are another underutilized gem on eBay. As a seller, you can create targeted coupons for specific products or categories in your store. These can be shared directly with buyers who have shown interest in your listings or with past customers to encourage repeat business. For new sellers, offering a limited-time coupon can be a smart way to build an initial customer base and create momentum for your store. The key to using coupons effectively is to make them time-sensitive, creating a sense of urgency that motivates buyers to act quickly.

Creating volume discounts is another strategy that can work wonders, especially if you're selling items that buyers might purchase in multiples. Offering deals like "buy two, get one free" or discounts for purchasing more than one item not only increases your sales per transaction but also encourages buyers to spend more in your store. This can be particularly effective when you're selling small, inexpensive items like accessories, office supplies, or craft materials. The psychological impact of getting a better deal when buying more can push buyers to make larger purchases than they originally intended.

Leveraging eBay's Promotions Manager is a crucial step in implementing these strategies. This tool allows you to create various types of promotions, including discounted shipping, order discounts, or bundle deals. For beginners, starting with simple promotions can help you understand buyer behavior and refine your approach. As you become more comfortable, you can experiment with different types of promotions to see which resonate best with your audience. Tracking the performance of these promotions is essential to understand what works and what doesn't, so you can continuously optimize your efforts.

Timing also plays a significant role in the effectiveness of your promotions. Running discounts and sales events during holidays, weekends, or shopping seasons can yield higher sales volumes. Buyers are more likely to shop during these periods, and having a well-timed promotion can make your listings stand out. Additionally, using countdown timers on sales or emphasizing the limited availability of discounts can create urgency, making buyers feel compelled to act before they miss out.

Customer communication is another element that shouldn't be ignored when using promotions and discounts. Highlighting your offers in your product descriptions, messaging buyers about upcoming sales, or even including details in your thank-you notes for past purchases can keep your promotions front and center. Engaging with your audience in this way builds trust and keeps your store top of mind when buyers are ready to shop again.

While the ultimate goal of using promotions and discounts is to drive sales, it's equally important to maintain a balance that ensures profitability. Offering discounts that are too steep or running promotions too frequently can eat into your profit margins. Instead, focus on strategic pricing that attracts buyers without undervaluing your products. By experimenting with different promotional tools and approaches, you can find the sweet spot that maximizes both sales volume and profit.

Leveraging eBay's Global Marketplace for Bigger Profits

As a beginner, you may think that focusing only on your local market is the best approach, but eBay offers a massive potential for growth and higher profits by expanding your reach to international buyers. The platform connects sellers to millions of customers worldwide, and when used strategically, this can significantly boost your sales.

By listing your products globally, you're no longer restricted to local demand. The global marketplace opens up a much larger audience with different tastes, needs, and purchasing power, which can translate into more sales. International buyers may have specific items they're looking for that aren't readily available in their local stores, which gives you a huge advantage if you can meet those needs.

Understanding the global audience and market is crucial. For example, some products may be more in demand in certain countries due to regional preferences or trends. If you're selling fashion, electronics, or collectibles, these markets could prove to be goldmines, with particular countries or regions showing higher interest in specific types of products. Buyers in countries like the United States, Canada, the UK, and Australia are often willing to pay premium prices for items that are either hard to find in their region or are less expensive abroad.

One of the key tools eBay provides for sellers looking to expand internationally is its Global Shipping Program (GSP). This program allows you to list items with worldwide shipping options, making it easier for international buyers to purchase from you. The Global Shipping Program works by having eBay handle the shipping logistics, duties, and customs, so you don't have to worry about managing these complex aspects of international shipping. This removes much of the hassle for sellers who are new to international sales and ensures that the buyer receives their product without additional delays or surprises.

The Global Shipping Program also has the added benefit of protecting you from certain risks associated with international sales. eBay takes on the responsibility of the shipping and customs process once the item reaches the U.S. shipping hub. This means you don't have to worry about lost items or complicated customs issues, which can often cause headaches for sellers.

If you're just starting out, one of the best ways to approach global selling is to start slow. Begin by targeting countries that speak the same language as you, such as the UK or Australia, as this reduces the risk of confusion with product descriptions or customer communication. As you gain confidence and experience with the platform, you can expand to more diverse markets, like Europe, Japan, or the Middle East.

While expanding to a global audience can increase your sales potential, there are also some key considerations to keep in mind. Shipping costs and delivery times can be higher and longer when shipping internationally. To account for this, it's essential to set up your shipping settings carefully, so you can offer competitive rates while factoring in the increased costs. You'll also need to ensure your product descriptions are clear, accurate, and free of language barriers that could deter potential buyers.

Another important aspect of selling globally is the currency exchange. eBay allows you to set up your store to accept payments in multiple currencies, which means you can automatically convert payments from buyers worldwide. However, it's important to keep track of exchange rates and consider them when pricing your products. If the exchange rate fluctuates, it may impact your profits, so staying on top of global currency trends can help you price your items effectively.

Additionally, providing excellent customer service becomes even more critical when selling internationally. Since buyers may be from different time zones, prompt communication is essential. Be prepared to answer questions quickly, offer detailed tracking information, and resolve issues that may arise with international shipments. A reputation for excellent customer service can set you apart from the competition and lead to positive feedback, which is crucial on eBay.

The eBay marketplace is also home to numerous international buyers who are looking for unique or specialty items that may not be available in their local market. This is a fantastic opportunity for you as a seller to source products with specific regional demands in mind. For instance, certain types of vintage or limited-edition items might be in higher demand in some countries, so by focusing on these niche markets, you can leverage the uniqueness of your inventory to attract buyers willing to pay a premium.

In some cases, using international selling to your advantage means thinking outside the box when it comes to sourcing products. You may find that what's considered a hot item in your local market is underpriced in other countries, and vice versa. By leveraging this information and adjusting your sourcing strategies accordingly, you can import products that are in demand overseas and export local products that may sell for a higher price abroad.

It's also worth noting that eBay's global marketplace includes a wide array of regional promotions, which sellers can participate in. These promotions often target specific countries or regions, so when you're listing globally, you can take advantage of these marketing opportunities. Participating in these promotions can help increase visibility for your products, leading to higher sales and broader exposure.

The Art of eBay Auctions

The essence of an eBay auction is its ability to create competition for your product. Auctions allow buyers to bid on an item, often leading to a final sale price higher than what you might expect through a fixed-price listing. However, there's an art to setting up an auction that will attract attention and drive up the final price. For a beginner, the first step is to understand the types of items that are most suitable for auctions. Auctions are ideal for products that have a sense of rarity or scarcity, or items that might have an enthusiastic following but aren't necessarily in high demand every day. If you're selling something with a niche appeal, like vintage collectibles, limited-edition items, or products that cater to a passionate community, auctions are a great way to tap into that enthusiasm.

A well-executed auction can bring in far more money than a fixed-price listing, but it also requires a good understanding of how to market the product effectively. Timing is critical when setting up an eBay auction. For instance, auctions that last seven days typically have the most success. A short auction window, such as three days, might generate too little interest, while an extended auction, like ten days, could lose the excitement needed to drive up bids. Seven days is usually long enough to reach a broad audience but short enough to keep the competitive tension high, ensuring that bidders are motivated to act quickly rather than waiting to see if prices will drop.

The starting price of your auction plays a significant role in its success. You might be tempted to start your auction at a low price to attract attention, but there's a delicate balance to maintain. Starting too low can lead to the item selling for far less than it's worth, while starting too high may scare off potential bidders. A common strategy is to start at a low price, even $0.99, to generate interest and let the bidding war begin, but only if you're comfortable with the potential risk of a lower final price. Alternatively, setting the starting price closer to the expected value can attract serious buyers who are willing to pay a fair price from the outset. If you're selling items that have a solid, well-understood market value, consider starting your auction at a price that reflects this value to avoid the risk of selling it for too little.

One of the most crucial elements of an eBay auction is the item description. Since auctions create urgency, potential buyers may make quick decisions based on the information they have in front of them. This makes it essential to provide detailed, accurate descriptions and high-quality photos. The more confident a buyer is in what they're purchasing, the more likely they are to bid. Take the time to capture clear images from different angles, highlighting any flaws or unique features. A well-detailed description with keywords relevant to the item's value will increase your visibility on eBay's search results. Using the right keywords can also help you capture the attention of buyers who may be specifically looking for your type of item.

The timing of your auction is just as important as the product itself. If you want your auction to generate maximum attention, consider starting it at a time when buyers are more likely to be online and actively bidding. Starting an auction in the middle of the night or during low-traffic periods can limit the number of potential buyers who see it. On the other hand, starting your auction during high-traffic times, such as evenings or weekends, increases the chances of receiving more bids. Even the time of day can make a difference; auctions that end in the evening tend to do better because buyers are home from work and have more time to engage with the auction.

Another critical factor in running a successful eBay auction is setting a reserve price. A reserve price is the minimum price you're willing to accept for your item, and it's hidden from the bidders until the auction ends. If the highest bid does not meet your reserve price, the auction ends without a sale. While it can offer peace of mind, it's important to set a reasonable reserve price that reflects the true market value of your item. Setting a reserve price too high may discourage bidding altogether, while setting it too low could result in you not getting the value you hoped for. For beginners, it's often wise to skip the reserve price and let the market determine what buyers are willing to pay. This can help you gauge the demand for your items and build confidence in your selling strategies.

Once your auction is live, it's essential to keep an eye on it and respond promptly to any questions or inquiries from potential buyers. If someone asks for more details or requests additional photos, be quick to respond. Bidders who feel like they have direct communication with the seller are more likely to place a bid.

Additionally, some sellers will use the "Buy It Now" option in conjunction with their auction listings, allowing buyers to skip the bidding process and buy the item at a fixed price if they prefer. This option can be a helpful strategy for attracting buyers who don't want to risk being outbid.

After the auction ends, if your item sells, the next step is to ensure a smooth transaction. Prompt communication and fast shipping are essential to maintaining a positive seller reputation. eBay places a significant emphasis on seller ratings, so providing excellent customer service is crucial to your long-term success. A smooth post-auction experience can encourage repeat customers and positive feedback, which, in turn, can drive more traffic to your future auctions.

Scaling Your Profits with eBay's Global Shipping Program

One of the most significant advantages of the GSP is that it allows you to sell internationally without needing to handle the logistics of international shipping yourself. Traditionally, selling to international customers would require you to calculate shipping costs for each destination, deal with customs forms, and navigate any language or currency barriers. This can feel overwhelming, especially if you're just starting your eBay journey. However, with the GSP, eBay takes care of these issues for you. All you need to do is ship your product to a domestic shipping center in the U.S. (or wherever your eBay account is registered), and eBay takes care of the rest, from international shipping to customs handling.

This makes it possible for you to focus on growing your business without worrying about the complexities of international shipping. Once the item arrives at eBay's domestic shipping center, they manage the shipping process, including international shipping fees and the necessary customs documentation. This ensures that your international buyers receive their items on time and without issues. The best part is that eBay automatically charges the buyer for the international shipping fees upfront, and you don't have to deal with collecting customs duties or taxes, which could be a significant headache otherwise.

By listing your items in the Global Shipping Program, you gain access to eBay's vast international marketplace, which opens the door to millions of potential buyers. It's not just about getting your items in front of customers in different countries; it's also about growing your brand's global presence. As more buyers from diverse countries find and purchase your products, your reputation as a seller increases. This can lead to even more sales in the future, as your eBay profile becomes known to international buyers looking for high-quality products.

For beginners, scaling your profits through the Global Shipping Program doesn't require a deep understanding of international logistics or substantial investment in infrastructure. You don't need to have an extensive knowledge of international shipping rules or even have access to shipping carriers that specialize in global services. With the GSP, eBay handles all of that for you, which reduces the barriers to entry and allows you to grow faster. Essentially, eBay gives you a set-it-and-forget-it approach to international sales, which is ideal for those just starting to build their eBay business.

Another major benefit of using the GSP is the transparency it offers. Buyers are clearly informed of the total cost of their purchase, including both the item price and the international shipping fees. This eliminates the uncertainty and surprise fees that can sometimes arise when dealing with international shipping on your own. This level of clarity builds trust with customers, which is crucial for maintaining a positive seller reputation, especially when you're just beginning your eBay selling journey. When buyers know exactly what they will be paying upfront, it reduces the likelihood of disputes, which can affect your seller rating.

For anyone serious about scaling their eBay business, the GSP offers access to markets that might have previously felt out of reach. Imagine the potential of selling your products to countries where your niche could be in high demand but where local access to your type of product is limited. For example, specialized home goods or unique fashion items could be highly sought after in international markets, where your specific offerings may not be readily available. With eBay's Global Shipping Program, your product can quickly gain traction in new markets, offering a more expansive customer base that could potentially drive sales beyond your initial expectations.

While expanding globally through the GSP is a fantastic opportunity, there are also a few things to consider when scaling your eBay business. You'll want to ensure your listings are well-crafted and appealing to international buyers, which means taking the time to use clear, concise descriptions and professional photos that showcase your products in the best light. Additionally, because buyers will be coming from different countries, it's important to ensure that your shipping times are realistic. While eBay handles the shipping logistics, delays can still happen due to customs, and you want to make sure you manage customer expectations around delivery times.

One of the most appealing aspects of eBay's Global Shipping Program is the simplicity it offers. As a beginner, you may be hesitant to take on international sales due to the complexity involved. However, with the GSP, you can confidently scale your profits without dealing with complicated shipping rules or the stress of managing international transactions. This program empowers you to focus on what really matters: sourcing great products, optimizing your listings, and delivering excellent customer service. By tapping into the global marketplace, you can significantly increase your revenue potential, positioning your eBay store for long-term success.

Chapter 9: Avoiding Common Pitfalls and Maximizing Profit

Mistakes Every New eBay Seller Makes and How to Avoid Them

1. Not Doing Enough Product Research

One of the most critical errors beginners make is listing products without thoroughly researching the market first. You might assume that because something is cheap or readily available, it will sell fast on eBay. However, not all products are in demand, and some may not sell for a price that covers your costs or generates a profit.

How to Avoid It

- **Research Demand:** Use eBay's completed listings to gauge how often an item sells and at what price. The "sold listings" filter will show you actual sale prices and help you assess the competitiveness of your product.

- **Evaluate Competition:** Look at what other sellers are offering. Are there too many similar items listed at lower prices? If so, can you add value by improving your listing, offering faster shipping, or adding better photos?

- **Use eBay's Tools:** Utilize eBay's research tools such as Terapeak (available for eBay store subscribers) to analyze historical sales data, trends, and prices for specific products.

2. Overpricing or Underpricing Products

Setting the wrong price is a rookie mistake. Either you overestimate the value of your product or undercut your competitors in an attempt to quickly make a sale, leading to lost profits or, worse, a lack of sales.

How to Avoid It

- **Competitive Pricing:** Research similar items in your category and price accordingly. Price too high, and you risk scaring away potential buyers; price too low, and you might miss out on profit.

- **Understand eBay's Fees:** Keep in mind that eBay charges seller fees, including listing and final value fees. Factor these into your pricing so you're still making a profit after these deductions.

- **Consider the Total Cost:** Don't forget to include shipping costs in your pricing. If you're offering free shipping, ensure the total price still covers your expenses.

3. Poor Listing Descriptions and Titles

A poorly written title or description can significantly decrease your chances of making a sale. Many beginners don't optimize their listings for search, leaving out relevant keywords, product details, or specific selling points that could attract buyers.

How to Avoid It:

- **Craft a Compelling Title:** Your title should be clear, descriptive, and packed with relevant keywords that buyers are likely to search for. Include important details like brand, size, model, condition, and color.

- **Use Keywords Effectively:** Think about what words your target audience would type into the search bar to find your product. Include those words naturally in both the title and the description.

- **Be Detailed and Honest in the Description:** Provide all relevant details about the product, including its condition, size, specifications, and any defects. If you're selling used items, make sure to mention any wear and tear.

4. Not Taking High-Quality Photos

A picture is worth a thousand words, especially on eBay. Low-quality or unclear photos can make your product appear less desirable, leading potential buyers to skip over your listing. Not providing multiple views or zoomed-in shots of important details can also be a deal-breaker.

How to Avoid It:

- **Take Clear, Well-Lit Photos:** Use a high-quality camera or smartphone to capture your items in bright, natural light. Avoid harsh shadows or cluttered backgrounds.

- **Show Multiple Angles:** Offer several photos from different angles to provide buyers with a comprehensive view of the item.

- **Highlight Key Features or Flaws:** If your product has a specific feature or defect, make sure it's visible in the photos. Transparency builds trust with buyers and can prevent returns.

5. **Ignoring Shipping Details**

Shipping is one of the most crucial aspects of eBay selling, and many beginners overlook important details like proper packaging, shipping costs, or delivery times. Mistakes in this area can lead to poor customer feedback, lost sales, or unexpected costs.

How to Avoid It:

- **Research Shipping Rates:** Use eBay's shipping calculator to determine the best shipping options and rates. Factor in the cost of packaging materials and shipping insurance if necessary.

- **Offer Multiple Shipping Options:** Buyers appreciate flexibility, so offer various shipping methods to suit different preferences, including economy and expedited shipping.

- **Package Items Carefully:** Ensure that your products are well-protected during transit to avoid damage. Poor packaging can lead to disputes, refunds, or negative feedback.

6. Neglecting Customer Service

Many new sellers underestimate the importance of excellent customer service. Poor communication or failure to address issues promptly can lead to unhappy buyers, negative feedback, and ultimately a decline in sales.

How to Avoid It:

- **Respond Promptly to Inquiries:** Be quick to respond to any buyer questions or concerns. Even a simple "thank you" or confirmation of the order goes a long way in building rapport.

- **Handle Disputes Professionally:** If a problem arises with a sale, approach it calmly and professionally. Always try to resolve the issue amicably, whether it's through a return, refund, or replacement.

- **Maintain a Positive Feedback Profile:** Encourage satisfied customers to leave positive feedback. This boosts your reputation and helps build trust with potential buyers.

7. Not Understanding eBay's Seller Policies and Fees

New sellers often ignore eBay's seller policies or don't fully understand how fees work. This can lead to unexpected costs, account restrictions, or even suspension.

How to Avoid It:

- **Read eBay's Seller Policies:** Familiarize yourself with eBay's selling rules, including listing guidelines, payment policies, and return procedures. Violating these policies can lead to account penalties.

- **Be Aware of eBay Fees:** Understand eBay's various fees (listing fees, final value fees, PayPal fees, etc.) and how they impact your profits. Ensure you're factoring these into your pricing and cost calculations.

8. Failing to Scale the Business

Some new sellers treat eBay as a side hobby and fail to scale their business when they see early success. Without proper planning and growth strategies, the business can stagnate.

How to Avoid It:

- **Reinvest Your Profits:** Consider reinvesting your profits back into sourcing more products or upgrading your eBay store to unlock additional features.

- **Automate Where Possible:** Use eBay's bulk listing tools and third-party software to streamline inventory management, order fulfillment, and other tasks.

- **Diversify Your Product Range:** As you grow, expand your offerings by adding new products or selling in different categories to attract a broader audience.

Managing Returns and Disputes Like a Pro

Managing returns and disputes on eBay is an inevitable part of selling, but how you handle these situations can significantly impact your success and reputation as a seller. One of the most important things to understand as a beginner is that returns and disputes aren't personal; they are simply part of doing business. The key is to approach them with professionalism, patience, and a clear strategy that protects both your interests and those of your buyers. When a return request comes through, the first step is to read the buyer's message carefully. Many times, the reason for the return is straightforward, such as an item not fitting their needs, a change of mind, or an issue with the product. It's important to respond promptly to maintain trust. eBay's metrics track how quickly you respond to such issues, and delays can affect your seller performance rating. Always be courteous in your communication, even if the request seems unreasonable. Buyers appreciate sellers who are willing to address their concerns, and a professional tone can often diffuse tension before it escalates into a dispute.

Understanding eBay's return policies is critical for managing these situations effectively. As a seller, you can set your return preferences, including the time frame for returns and whether you offer free return shipping. While offering free returns may seem like an added expense, it can lead to increased buyer confidence and potentially higher sales. However, it's important to weigh this against your profit margins. If a return request cites a legitimate issue, such as a defective product or an error in the listing, it's usually best to accept the return quickly and provide a prepaid shipping label if required. This not only resolves the issue efficiently but also demonstrates that you value your customers' satisfaction.

For disputes, the stakes can feel higher, especially if a buyer escalates the issue to eBay's Resolution Center. It's essential to gather all relevant information about the transaction before responding. Review the original listing, the buyer's messages, and any photos or evidence they may have provided. If you have tracking information showing that the item was delivered as promised, provide this to eBay during the dispute process. Transparency and clear documentation are your best allies in resolving disputes in your favor. When the buyer's claim seems questionable, maintain a calm and factual tone. Avoid accusing the buyer of dishonesty, as this can escalate the situation further. Instead, focus on presenting evidence that supports your case.

Preventing returns and disputes starts long before a sale is made. Clear and accurate product descriptions are your first line of defense. Take the time to highlight any flaws or imperfections in used items and provide detailed measurements, specifications, and high-quality photos from multiple angles. Buyers who know exactly what they're purchasing are less likely to file a return or dispute. Shipping also plays a critical role. Always use reliable carriers and include tracking on every shipment. This not only protects you in the case of "item not received" claims but also reassures buyers that their purchase is on its way. For high-value items, consider adding insurance for extra protection. Packaging is another area where attention to detail can prevent issues. Properly securing items for transit reduces the risk of damage, which is a common cause of returns.

Sometimes, a buyer may request a return for a reason you believe is unfounded, such as claiming the item is not as described when it matches the listing perfectly. In these cases, it's still important to remain professional. If eBay decides in favor of the buyer, the best course of action is to accept the return and move on. While it may feel frustrating in the moment, focusing on the bigger picture is crucial. Your long-term success on eBay depends on maintaining a positive seller rating and avoiding negative feedback.

Dealing with negative feedback is another aspect of managing disputes effectively. If a buyer leaves negative feedback after a return or dispute, you can reach out to them through eBay's messaging system to see if they are willing to revise it. Politely ask if there's anything you can do to resolve the issue and make them feel better about their experience. Sometimes, offering a small gesture, like a partial refund or discount on a future purchase, can turn an unhappy buyer into a repeat customer. If the feedback is unjustified or violates eBay's policies, you can request its removal through eBay's Feedback Removal Tool.

One of the most challenging aspects of managing returns and disputes is balancing the cost of resolving issues with maintaining your profit margins. For low-cost items, it may be more economical to offer a refund without requiring the item to be returned. This approach can save on return shipping costs and time spent processing the return. For higher-value items, it's worth taking a more structured approach, including requiring buyers to provide photos of the issue before approving a return. This step not only verifies the claim but also discourages fraudulent returns.

How to Stay Ahead of Trends and Evolving Market Conditions

Keeping an eye on popular culture, social media, and global events can provide valuable insights. For example, the launch of a new blockbuster movie, a viral social media trend, or a major sporting event can spark demand for specific items. Pay close attention to influencers and celebrities who often set trends, as their choices frequently drive consumer behavior. Similarly, monitor seasonal and holiday trends, as these can create short-term but lucrative opportunities for sellers who prepare in advance. Halloween, Christmas, and back-to-school periods all present unique selling prospects, and being ready with the right inventory can give you an edge.

Data is your best friend when it comes to identifying and capitalizing on trends. eBay itself offers tools like the Terapeak Research platform, which provides insights into what's currently selling, how often, and at what price points. Regularly analyzing this data will help you identify products that are gaining popularity and understand pricing patterns that allow you to remain competitive. Beyond eBay's tools, you can use platforms like Google Trends to track search interest for particular items over time. A product with a rising interest curve might indicate an emerging trend, and getting in early can lead to significant profits before the market becomes saturated.

Staying ahead also means being adaptable with your inventory. As a beginner, it might feel safe to focus on a narrow range of products, but flexibility is key to long-term success. If you notice that certain categories are becoming less popular or oversaturated with competition, it's important to pivot quickly. This might involve diversifying your product offerings or shifting focus to a different niche altogether. Don't let emotional attachment to a specific type of product prevent you from moving on when the demand dwindles. Successful sellers remain fluid and open to change, always looking for the next big opportunity.

Networking with other sellers and joining online communities can also be incredibly beneficial. Many experienced sellers share their insights about trending products, sourcing strategies, and market conditions. Participating in forums, Facebook groups, or even attending seller conferences can expose you to ideas you may not have considered. Collaboration often leads to innovative approaches and fresh perspectives, helping you stay ahead of competitors who operate in isolation.

Another strategy involves observing your direct competition. Study their listings, pricing strategies, and product descriptions to see what they are doing successfully. If you notice a competitor consistently selling out of certain items, it could signal a trend worth exploring. However, don't just copy; look for ways to improve upon their offerings, whether it's through better customer service, faster shipping times, or more appealing product bundles.

Technological advancements also play a significant role in shaping market conditions. For instance, emerging trends in sustainable and eco-friendly products have gained traction as consumers become more environmentally conscious. Staying informed about these broader societal shifts can help you identify products that align with changing values. Similarly, advancements in technology, such as smart home devices or wearables, often create new categories of products that quickly rise in demand. The sellers who recognize these opportunities early are the ones who reap the most significant rewards.

Experimentation is another powerful tool for staying ahead. Testing new products, listing strategies, and pricing models allows you to gather firsthand data about what works and what doesn't. Don't be afraid to take calculated risks by investing in small quantities of a trending product to gauge its performance. This approach minimizes potential losses while giving you the chance to capitalize on emerging trends. Over time, you'll develop a sharper intuition for recognizing profitable opportunities.

Building strong supplier relationships can also be a game-changer. When you have reliable sources for inventory, you can react more quickly to changing trends. Some suppliers may even provide insights into what's selling well in different markets, giving you an inside track on emerging opportunities. This becomes particularly important when dealing with high-demand products where speed is crucial. Being able to secure inventory faster than your competitors can give you a decisive advantage.

Chapter 10: Creating Passive Income on eBay

How to Transition to Passive Income with eBay

A key aspect of transitioning to passive income lies in choosing the right products to sell. Some products naturally lend themselves to a more passive model, particularly items that are easy to source, ship, and replenish. These are often evergreen products—items with consistent demand regardless of season or trends. Think of things like replacement parts, office supplies, or certain types of clothing that are always in style. By focusing on these types of products, you can avoid the volatility of trendy or seasonal items that require constant monitoring and adjustment.

Another essential element is creating systems that automate as many aspects of your eBay business as possible. Listing items is one of the most time-consuming parts of running an eBay store, but there are tools available to simplify this process. Third-party software can be used to bulk upload listings, optimize titles and descriptions, and even automate pricing adjustments to stay competitive. This allows you to create a catalog of products quickly and efficiently, saving you hours of work. Additionally, automating inventory management ensures that you're never caught off guard by stock shortages or overselling, which can lead to dissatisfied customers and lost profits.

Shipping is another area where efficiency can transform your eBay business into a more passive model. Offering free shipping with preset packaging options can streamline your process. Investing in shipping software that integrates with eBay can help you print labels in bulk and track shipments with ease. Even better, consider partnering with a fulfillment service or exploring eBay's Global Shipping Program. These services handle much of the logistical side of shipping for you, reducing your workload significantly. This kind of setup allows you to focus more on sourcing and scaling your business rather than being bogged down by daily shipping tasks.

Building a reliable supply chain is a critical component of sustaining a passive income business. This involves developing relationships with wholesalers, manufacturers, or dropshipping suppliers who can fulfill orders consistently and with minimal input from you. Dropshipping, in particular, can be a game-changer when it comes to passive income. In this model, you never handle the inventory directly. Instead, your supplier ships products directly to your customers. While the profit margins may be slimmer compared to handling inventory yourself, the tradeoff in terms of reduced time and effort can be worth it. With dropshipping, your role is primarily to manage listings, customer inquiries, and occasional supplier communication, allowing you to focus on growth.

Customer service is another area where the right systems can make a huge difference. Maintaining high feedback ratings and ensuring quick response times to inquiries are crucial for your long-term success on eBay. However, this doesn't mean you have to handle every message and issue personally. Many sellers use templates for frequently asked questions and common scenarios, which can significantly reduce the time spent on customer interactions. eBay's automated response options can also handle some of these tasks for you, ensuring customers get timely replies even when you're not actively managing your store.

Once these foundational systems are in place, the next step is scaling your eBay business to maximize its passive income potential. This often involves expanding your product catalog, diversifying your niches, and leveraging data to identify new opportunities. Analyzing your sales metrics can reveal which products perform best, allowing you to double down on high-performing categories while phasing out less profitable ones. Over time, this refinement process helps you create a streamlined and profitable store that requires minimal ongoing effort to maintain.

Expanding your reach to international markets can further enhance your income potential. eBay's Global Shipping Program simplifies the process of selling to customers worldwide, handling customs and international shipping for you. By enabling this feature, you can tap into a larger customer base without taking on the complexities of international logistics yourself. This approach not only boosts sales but also helps your business become more resilient to changes in local market conditions.

Delegating tasks is another effective way to transition to a more passive model. Hiring a virtual assistant or part-time employee to handle routine tasks like listing creation, customer communication, or order management can free up your time to focus on high-level strategies. Outsourcing doesn't have to be expensive, and the time savings can make a significant difference in how passive your income becomes. As your business grows, you may even consider hiring someone to manage the entire operation, allowing you to step back almost entirely.

Using eBay's Automation Features to Make Money While You Sleep

One of the most practical automation tools on eBay is the ability to schedule listings. Instead of manually uploading products throughout the day, sellers can create multiple listings in advance and schedule them to go live at specific times. This feature is especially beneficial when targeting buyers across different time zones or capitalizing on peak shopping hours. For example, if you want your listings to appear when buyers are most active, scheduling ensures that your products are front and center without requiring you to be online at odd hours.

Another powerful feature is eBay's automatic relisting option, which is a lifesaver for unsold items. When a product doesn't sell, manually relisting it can become a tedious task. By enabling automatic relisting, your unsold items are reposted without any effort on your part. This ensures that your products remain visible to potential buyers, increasing the chances of a sale over time. For beginners, this can be a game-changer, as it reduces the likelihood of listings being forgotten or left inactive.

Pricing is another area where automation can significantly impact your sales. eBay offers tools like automatic pricing adjustments, which allow you to set parameters for your item's price to adjust based on market conditions or competition. For example, if other sellers lower their prices on a similar product, eBay's automation can adjust your price to remain competitive, helping you win the coveted "Buy It Now" spot or attract more bidders in auctions. Conversely, if demand surges and competitors raise their prices, your listing price can increase accordingly, maximizing your profits without any manual input.

Shipping, often seen as one of the more time-consuming aspects of selling, can also be streamlined through automation. eBay allows you to create predefined shipping policies that automatically apply to your listings. By setting rules for domestic and international shipping, handling times, and return policies, you save yourself the trouble of inputting this information every time you list a product. For sellers with a wide range of items, this can save hours of work and ensure consistency across all listings. Paired with eBay's bulk shipping label printing feature, you can handle orders in batches, reducing the time spent preparing packages for delivery.

Customer communication is another area where automation shines. eBay's messaging system allows you to create custom templates for responding to common buyer inquiries. Whether it's a question about shipping times, product details, or return policies, these templates enable you to provide quick, professional responses without having to type out a reply each time. Additionally, automated feedback tools can leave positive reviews for buyers after a transaction is completed, fostering goodwill and encouraging them to return for future purchases.

For sellers looking to scale their businesses, eBay offers third-party integrations that take automation to the next level. Tools like Sellbrite and InkFrog allow you to manage inventory, sync listings across multiple platforms, and analyze sales data—all from a single dashboard. These integrations make it easier to expand your reach and manage larger inventories without feeling overwhelmed. They also provide valuable insights into which products are performing well, enabling you to make data-driven decisions that enhance profitability.

One often-overlooked feature is the use of eBay's promotions and markdown tools. These allow you to set up automated discounts, such as offering a percentage off after a buyer adds multiple items to their cart. By creating these promotions, you not only encourage larger orders but also provide buyers with an incentive to choose your store over competitors. eBay's promotional tools can run in the background, working tirelessly to boost your sales even when you're not actively managing your store.

Automation also extends to inventory management, which is critical for maintaining a successful eBay business. Running out of stock on popular items can result in missed sales and disappointed customers. By using inventory tracking tools, you can set alerts or even automate restocking through dropshipping partnerships or wholesale suppliers. These systems ensure that your store remains stocked with in-demand products, keeping your sales pipeline steady and reliable.

Leveraging Dropshipping for Easy Profits

One of the biggest appeals of dropshipping is its accessibility. As a beginner, you might feel overwhelmed by the thought of purchasing stock and worrying about whether it will sell. Dropshipping removes that risk entirely. You only pay for a product after you've already made a sale, which ensures you aren't sitting on unsold inventory. This approach allows you to test a variety of products and niches without committing to large quantities. It's a perfect way to experiment and discover what works best on eBay, especially if you're still finding your footing as a seller.

The key to success with dropshipping on eBay lies in selecting the right products and suppliers. Choosing reliable suppliers is non-negotiable. You want to work with partners who not only provide quality products but also have a track record of timely shipping and excellent customer service. When your supplier delivers on their promises, it reflects positively on you as a seller. Any delays, damaged items, or customer complaints caused by the supplier will ultimately fall on your shoulders, so due diligence in this area is essential. Platforms like AliExpress, CJ Dropshipping, and SaleHoo are popular choices among eBay dropshippers because they offer a wide range of products and competitive prices.

Pricing is another crucial aspect of dropshipping. Since you're not purchasing products in bulk, the per-item cost is often higher compared to wholesale pricing. This means you need to be strategic about your pricing to ensure a healthy profit margin while remaining competitive on eBay. Research your competitors to see how they price similar items and aim to strike a balance between affordability and profitability. Don't undervalue your time and effort; your pricing should reflect the value you bring to the table, such as well-optimized listings, fast response times to customer inquiries, and a seamless shopping experience.

Another important element to master is crafting compelling listings that attract buyers. Since you won't be handling the products directly, you'll rely heavily on the product descriptions and images provided by your suppliers. However, it's rarely a good idea to copy and paste this information directly onto your eBay listing. To stand out in a crowded marketplace, you need to customize your product descriptions, highlighting the features and benefits in a way that speaks directly to your target audience. Use high-quality images, and if possible, order samples of the products to take your own photos.

This adds an extra layer of authenticity and allows you to verify the quality of what you're selling.

Shipping times can be a potential challenge in dropshipping, especially when working with international suppliers. Many customers on eBay expect fast shipping, and long delivery times can deter buyers or lead to negative feedback. To address this, be transparent about shipping timelines in your listings and consider focusing on suppliers who offer faster shipping options. Some dropshipping platforms even have warehouses in multiple countries, which can significantly reduce shipping times for certain regions. Communicating effectively with your customers about what to expect can go a long way in managing their satisfaction and building trust.

Customer service plays a vital role in dropshipping success. Since you're not directly in control of the shipping and handling process, maintaining excellent communication with your buyers is essential. If a customer has an issue with their order, they'll come to you for resolution, even if the problem originated with the supplier. Being proactive, responsive, and solution-oriented can help you navigate these challenges and maintain a positive reputation on eBay. Remember, happy customers are more likely to leave positive feedback and return for future purchases, which is invaluable for growing your business.

Scaling your dropshipping business is relatively straightforward once you've identified what sells well. By analyzing your sales data, you can focus on high-performing products and expand your inventory within that niche. You might even consider creating an eBay store to build your brand and increase customer loyalty. As your business grows, you can also explore working with multiple suppliers to diversify your product offerings and reduce the risk of relying on a single source.

One of the most exciting aspects of dropshipping is its potential for long-term profitability. While it's an excellent model for beginners, it can also serve as the foundation for a larger e-commerce business. By starting with dropshipping on eBay, you gain valuable experience in product research, pricing strategies, and customer service. Over time, you might decide to branch out into other platforms or even transition to a hybrid model that combines dropshipping with stocking high-demand items. The skills you develop while dropshipping are transferable, equipping you with the tools to succeed in various e-commerce ventures.

Conclusion

Congratulations! You've made it to the end of this guide, and I hope you're feeling excited and confident about starting your eBay selling journey. Whether you're here to make a little extra cash on the side, create a thriving business from home, or build a full-fledged reselling empire, you now have the tools, strategies, and insights to make it happen.

Selling on eBay can feel overwhelming at first, and that's perfectly okay. Every successful seller started where you are right now—unsure, curious, and eager to learn. The good news is, you don't have to know everything or get it all perfect from the start. Success on eBay isn't about perfection; it's about persistence. Each listing, sale, and customer interaction is a chance to learn and improve.

Remember, the key to succeeding on eBay is to stay consistent and adaptable. Trends will change, challenges will arise, and competition will always be there. But if you keep researching, testing, and refining your approach, you'll find what works best for you. This isn't just about making money—it's about building something you can take pride in.

Also, don't forget to enjoy the process. There's something incredibly rewarding about finding that perfect product, making a great sale, or receiving positive feedback from a happy customer. Those moments are what make the effort worthwhile.

If there's one final piece of advice I can leave you with, it's this: take action. Reading this book is a great first step, but the real progress happens when you dive in and start listing, selling, and experimenting. Even if you make mistakes—and you will—they're simply part of the journey to success.

So, go out there and make it happen! Your first sale is waiting, your first happy customer is ready, and your future as a successful eBay seller is yours to create. I can't wait to hear about the incredible results you'll achieve.

Here's to your success and the journey ahead. Happy selling!

Printed in Great Britain
by Amazon